Natural Control of
Garden Pests

*To Bryan and Edward and the other
inhabitants of my garden*

NATURAL CONTROL

OF

Garden Pests

Jackie French

Aird Books
Melbourne

Aird Books Pty Ltd
PO Box 122
Flemington, Vic. 3031
Phone (03) 376 4461

First published by Aird Books in 1990
Reprinted 1993

National Library of Australia
Cataloguing-in-publication data

French, Jacqueline.
  Natural control of garden pests

  Includes index.
  ISSBN 0 947214 13 5

  1. Garden pests-Australia—Control. 2. Organic
  gardening—Australia. I. Title.

635.04995

Design by Pauline McClenahan, Bookworks
Cover illustrations by Greg Jorgenson
Photographs by Jackie French
Typesetting and layout by Midland Typesetters,
  Maryborough, Victoria
Printed by Australian Print Group,
  Maryborough, Victoria

CONTENTS

INTRODUCTION

Pesticide sprays do not make healthy gardens, nor do organic sprays. This is a book about natural pest control. That is, about how to have a flourishing garden (or orchard or market garden) without the need for sprays. It gives advice on organic methods of pest control, by the use of pesticides and fungicides made from natural ingredients, which break down quickly and become harmless. You may use these natural methods of control while you improve your soil and garden design, the real foundations of good growing.

Most pests need to be controlled; not eradicated. If your impossible-to-live-with great-aunt Gladys planned to visit you, you wouldn't get out the arsenic. You'd find some way of discouraging her before she came. Even 'environmentally friendly' sprays are not a long-term answer. There's no point being 'friendly' to the environment: we are part of the environment, not separate from it. It makes as much sense to be friendly to your foot. We simply need to find our own place, to live within the world, not reorganise it; to learn to grow our food according to environmental constraints, so that 'remedies' aren't needed.

Unfortunately, when people ask 'How do you control such and such?' they are looking for a 'spray-with-x-or-y' answer. We've been conditioned to think that only sprays will cure our pest problems. We go on with the same garden designs and regimes as the last century in Europe: neat rows, well-dug soil, early planting, regular spraying for pests. These are all good ways to increase pests in your garden.

Pesticides are bandaids, not cures. Yet since World War II we have been propagandised to believe that they are necessary for growing our food and protecting our gardens. Because of this we tolerate pesticide disasters, harmful residues, growing pesticide resistance, and growing chemical overkill, which is often caused by the routine use of 'preventative' pesticides.

Why not use pesticides? Most of the bad pesticide publicity has been about their effects on human health, about species wiped out as pesticides travel up the food chain. Yet from the gardening and farming standpoint also, pesticides can have horrendous consequences. Pesticides can cause pest increases instead of controlling them, by wiping out the natural predators that previously kept them in check. Pesticides also create new pest species. The light-brown apple-moth, for example, became a pest only when wide-spread use of DDT wiped out the natural enemies that had formerly controlled it. CSIRO research into soybean pests has shown that if spraying kills off natural enemies along with pests, pest populations may become even larger than in untreated areas. Unfortunately we rarely realise that a spray at the aphids in early spring may mean more pests later in summer.

Instead of pesticides, we need healthy soil and an understanding of the processes we are interfering with. Instead of trying to eliminate pests, we should simply try to manage them, or manage ourselves and our growing techniques. There is no point in killing off every cabbage-white caterpillar if you need to kill only 80 per cent to save your crop. The remaining 20 per cent will feed the predators that will survive to control them in future.

Why, then, are pesticides used? Firstly, because of bad management. Poor farm or garden design can lead to pest outbreaks, which can, like grasshopper plagues, spread over thousands of kilometres. Secondly, pesticides are big business. They make money, and our 'need' for them is artificially promoted. Thirdly, we have been conditioned to think of all insects (harmful or not) as enemies, to reach for the spray can when we see one. Fourthly, glossy, plasticised, artificially coloured supermarket food has made us intolerant of even the tiniest blemish on our food.

I love food. I love the way it tastes naturally, sun-warm from the garden, not bland in a supermarket tray. I love the way it looks, its infinite variety, not the stereotype of pure red glossy apples (brown and mealy inside their wax) and coloured oranges that taste of rotting peel. I'm not prepared to sacrifice my joy in any of these to fit in with the sterile images of colour and gloss. I am not prepared to accept that pollution and poisons are needed to grow good food. I want to share the world and my garden with the complexities and joys of other species: mammal, insect, reptile. A garden should be a place of growing things, not of destruction.

This book is dedicated to those who try to understand their gardens, who work with them, who don't see every insect as an enemy and every problem to be matched with a prepackaged answer on the garden-centre shelves. It is a book for people who love their gardens and the world.

CHAPTER 1

A Problem-free Garden

NATURAL PEST CONTROL

Natural pest control is designing a garden or farming system so that it does not need pesticides, organic or otherwise. There are five things you need for a pest-free garden. All are linked. The first four are: good soil; healthy garden design; as little stress as possible for your plants; and predators, to keep the pest-levels naturally controlled. The fifth one is harder. It is a change in attitude. It means not dashing out with a can of poison to attack every insect in the garden; it means learning to wait and to watch; it means revising your idea that all pests are necessarily bad.

We have been conditioned to think of any insect as a pest, whether it causes damage to plants or not. We spray as a preventative measure, using spraying calendars, believing that if we don't get them first, they'll get us. The ideal for many gardeners is an ecological desert, inhabited only by humans and their domesticated species. Fortunately this dream can never become a reality. But a lot of damage can be done in trying to achieve it.

What you *do not* want in your garden is a seasonal invasion of insects, so that irrevocable damage is done to your plants before predator numbers can build up to cope with them. What you need is a regular supply of predator food (of course, these need not be pest species), so that you have a base population of predators to build up in response to pest numbers; or a large number of predators, such as birds, that can move from one diet to another as insect populations vary.

But 'pests' have other roles. The sugary secretions of aphids and other sap-suckers, when washed to the ground, may stimulate nitrogen-fixing bacteria. 'Hungry' plants may even attract sap-sucking insects. Even nematodes, often seen only as garden pests, can help reduce pest problems. Many nematodes parasitise and help to control a wide range of insects, multiplying inside the insect carcass. Nematodes will soon be released commercially as controllers of pests such as strawberry weevil, banana scab moth, scarab beetle larvae, and rice-stem borer. Various fungi feed on eelworm, which is a pest of roots and stalks.

One of the best natural controls of the sirex wasp (which threatens pine plantations) is an introduced nematode, *Deladenus*. This nematode may control wasp numbers, so it is not a commercial threat. Trials by the Tasmanian Department of Agriculture and CSIRO have shown that a spray of nematodes will give 95 per cent control of currant-stem borer. Chemical fumigation only gives 80 per cent control.

Mites need not be sap-suckers. Predatory mites can control leaf-eating mites and pests such as aphids, mealy-bugs and whiteflies. The *Typhlodromus* predatory mites are useful in commercial orchards, because they are relatively resistant to insecticides.

Armillaria fungi grow on old tree stumps and spread through the roots to afflict other trees. But if other fungi attack the tree first, the competition excludes *Armillaria*. Root-knot nematode is attacked by the parasite *Pasteuria*. CSIRO and the Queensland Department of Primary Industries are investigating ways of commercially exploiting this.

Pear and cherry slug is another example. More cherries are killed by too much care than too little. Cherries do best with little added feeding, and fruit for years on the same wood. Too much nitrogen means too many leaves, which shade fruit and make it rot. Fruit from an over-fertilised tree tends to split before it is quite ripe. Trees infested with pear and cherry slug lose a lot of their leaves, a natural method of cutting back over-lush growth. In a natural orchard, predation controls the pest before it can do irreversible harm to the tree.

Many modern 'improved' plant species are more pest prone than older species. Many have been developed to take maximum advantage of high rates of water and artificial fertiliser: soft, sappy growth that needs similar doses of pesticides to survive. Even apparently harmless modifications, such as breeding apple trees that bear consistently from year to year instead of once every second year, may increase pest problems. An apple tree that bears only every second year helps to starve pests such as codling moth. Pests also help to cull out weak specimens. Pests really are attracted to unhealthy plants. Don't tolerate weak plants in your garden: root them out. Either they are naturally weak specimens, or the site is wrong for them. Weak plants will attract pests, and pathogens may possibly spread from them to other plants.

Christmas beetles and leafminers may defoliate gum trees; but this attack may be useful, by helping to recycle the nutrients in old leaves back into the soil and then to the tree for new growth. Termites may hollow out old trees; but these hollows attract nesting birds, and the droppings help fertilise the tree. The birds may also keep down insect pests that might further stress the tree.

Most pest control isn't done by people. If nothing ate the scale in your back garden (and there is almost certainly some scale there, perhaps not enough to notice) you might be knee deep by Christmas.

This doesn't happen. In fact, in most cases you don't realise you have a pest, because the predators keep the numbers under control. Even in the most insect-free garden, agencies other than humans control pest numbers: predators, parasites, weather, plant health, territory space.

At best we only understand a few of the complex relationships around us. Attempts to control them may lead to disaster. Instead, we need to learn to work with the processes around us, and to interfere as little as possible.

Good soil

It took me nearly a decade of farming to accept that healthy soil means healthy plants. Plants in good soil are far less pest-prone, and even if they are attacked by pests they usually recover satisfactorily. If you have pest problems in your garden, improve your soil with mulch and compost. This seems too simple to be effective, especially in a world where problems have to be cured with sprays and other commercial products. It is also a long-term solution, and quick-fix solutions are more attractive.

My vegetable garden grows in an old depleted orchard. It needed feeding. So this year half my silver beet was spread with compost. I gave well-rotted hen manure to the rest. The compost-fed silver beet grew steadily through winter, without pests or blemishes. Leaf spot disappeared. The plot fed with hen manure didn't grow at all in the cold weather, was badly infested with leaf spot and later with caterpillars in spring.

Late in winter a wallaby broke into the garden. It ate the composted silver beet, and left the rest. Wallabies are no fools. Well-fed crops may be less prone to insect damage, but mammalian and bird pests prefer them.

I have watched pest-filled gardens on poor soil gradually become relatively pest-free (or at least free of intolerable pest damage) when the soil is improved. This is partly because well-fed plants seem to be less attractive to pests. It is also because well-fed plants outgrow small amounts of pest damage.

A good spring application of high-nitrogen fertiliser plus a lot of water is the best way I know to attract pests and disease. High-nitrogen fertilisers promote soft, green, sappy growth and weak bark, which attract pests.

Try this yourself. Make two garden plots. Plant the same things in each. Feed one lot with compost and the other with any proprietary 'complete plant food'. Count the pests on each. Even if the plants are next to each other, you will find dramatic differences.

Compost and mulch also help control plant disease, as well as pest problems. Compost can kill pest pathogens or inhibit them (for example, phytophthera and other root-rots, potato scab, various harmful nematodes) and break down harmful herbicide or pesticide residues.

I make very little compost, preferring simply to leave the composting materials on the soil as mulch to rot down themselves. This is sometimes called 'sheet composting'. It is a lot less work than a compost heap. Yet I have no doubt that properly made compost is far more effective in both feeding the plants and preventing pest and disease problems. I just don't get round to making enough of it, and sheet compost is better than no compost.

A classic compost heap

Compost needs moisture, heat, nitrogen and air. A compost heap should be moist, but not wet, and placed in a warm spot, preferably under the broken shade of a tree.

To decompose quickly, compost needs nitrogen. To every layer of compost add something like blood and bone, hen manure, urine or fresh grass clippings. The carbon-nitrogen ratio of compost is one of the most important aspects to be considered. Sawdust, for example, has a low carbon-nitrogen ratio, and will take a long time to decompose without large amounts of added nitrogen. Hen manure has a high carbon-nitrogen ratio, but valuable nitrogen can be lost as ammonia if it isn't mixed with a low-nitrogen material.

If your heap gets too hot, and the inside burns to ash, it probably has too much nitrogen. Keep turning it until it cools down. If it fails to heat up, you don't have enough nitrogen. Mix hen manure or blood and bone or urine with water and pour it over the heap. Check again a few days later to see if you need more.

The micro-organisms in compost also need phosphorus for rapid decomposition. This doesn't matter if you are using kitchen waste for backyard compost, as most commercial vegetable crops are grown with superphosphate, which you will be recycling for your garden. But the materials for your large-scale compost may be phosphorus-deficient if you are using woody residues. In such a case add a sprinkle of bone meal or ground rock phosphate. Never do more than sprinkle. Phosphorus over 2 per cent of weight will inhibit decomposition.

The more the material in your compost heap is shredded, the faster it will decompose. I put the more solid of ours (blackberry stalks mostly, and thicker prunings) through an old chaff-cutter. If you have a slasher on your tractor, you can run it over a few times. Give your compost air by turning it. Or make 'chimneys' by building the pile around stakes and pulling them out later.

If you follow these rules you should get good, fast compost.

Compost activators should be unnecessary because good compost is very fast. But if you want to try an activator, add a sprig of yarrow, or a spadeful of soil from underneath yarrow, a handful of chamomile flowers, or layers of comfrey leaves. Compost made under the drip line of an elder tree is said to do well.

Compost is slightly acidic. Never add lime, because it will accelerate nitrogen loss. Remember that the problem with acid soil is the unavailability of nutrients, not the acidity itself. You may well find that this doesn't matter in compost-enriched soil, where elements tend to be made more available to plants anyway.

A large-scale compost heap

Drive stakes into the ground in a line about a metre apart. Remove the grass around them, or sprinkle some old compost: this is to facilitate the entry of natural 'starters' present in soil or compost.

Pile on the coarsest material you have, such as branches or corn stalks. Add a hand-span of green matter. Add some nitrogenous material, such as blood and bone or hen manure, or a wider band of cow or horse manure. Now add more green matter, a thin layer of soil, and repeat. Make the pile all in one go if you can.

A large-scale compost heap should be no more than 1.5 metres high, but can be as long as you want.

Take out the stakes. These will be ventilation chimneys. Now water until it is moist, and turn every three or four days. You can use a tractor with a bucket for this, or do it by hand. It may not be necessary if there is enough air trapped in the coarse bottom layer and the chimneys. Water if it is dry and add more nitrogenous material if it fails to heat up after a week.

The compost should be ready in six weeks. Finely chopped materials and good conditions may give you compost in a week. Very large mounds may take three months to mature.

Check your compost every week and speed it up (if it is slow) with moisture or nitrogen or turning.

Simple compost

There are several bins on the market where you just throw in everything and wait. This is a slow way of making compost, but the result can still be good. Other easy methods include the garbage bag method: bung your scraps (especially fruit-fly or codling-moth infected fruit) into a thick garbage bag, seal it, and leave it in the sun until you can no longer feel the shapes of original components. Open it and use. It will stink, but only for a couple of hours.

Kitchen compost can be made by filling a bucket with kitchen scraps, and adding a layer of coarse dry grass clippings or sawdust to soak up the liquid. When the bucket is full, up-end it on the ground so the fluid flows out, and wait at least two months for it to decompose.

How much compost?

It is impossible to over-fertilise with compost. Poor soils may need 10 kg per square metre, but 3 kg per square metre may be a good maintenance regime for fertile soils. But if you don't have enough, use what you have, and add other fertilisers, mulches, etc., to make up the difference.

Artificial fertilisers

Small amounts of artificial fertiliser do not do much harm, and when plants are starving may do a lot of good, if you can't get anything else. But never give too much, and never as a matter of routine. As well as promoting pest and disease problems, artificial fertilisers can be quickly leached away. They are expensive, can cause cancer-promoting nitrites in food, and may burn off micro-life. Artificial fertilisers can lead you to bad habits if you add them as quick fixes instead of organising a more stable, recycling fertility regime. Avoid them.

Soil pH

Some pest and disease problems seem to be associated with soil pH. Common potato scab is a problem in alkaline soils. Springtails and clubroot are worst in acid soils. But remember that it is not the acidity and alkalinity as such that cause plant problems. It is simply that in acid and alkaline soil certain nutrients are more available. An 'active' soil or one fertilised with good compost should increase the nutrients available to your plants, even if it is slightly too acid or alkaline.

A healthy garden

A healthy garden is one that is suited to your area. Plant according to shade, sun, air, drainage, competition. There may be a few 'pets' among them, plants that you are fond of and need cosseting (like our banana tree), but the backbone will be strong, well-placed plants. Concentrate on survivors.

Encourage diversity. This doesn't mean a thousand varieties of roses or peaches. Most severe pest outbreaks are associated with large monocultures (grass can be a monoculture). If there are many similar plants growing together of the same age and same type, pests can spread and build up very quickly. Diversity can simply be a mechanical way of preventing this.

Monocultures also mean regular ploughing, complete change-overs of crops, and loss of whatever stability is building up.

Create stable conditions for pests and predators throughout the year. Have established perennials in your garden as well as a number of plants going to seed throughout the year, as a year-round food source for pests and their predators. One of the first rules of natural pest control is having a constant, small population of pests for a small resident population of predators. When seasonal or other change occurs the first builds up and the second will follow.

Avoid plant stress. Some years ago I planted seventy peach trees in an orchard. Three months later, two were attacked by aphids; then by two-spotted mites; the next year they had curly leaf. But only those two trees. The other sixty-eight, while somewhat wallaby-eaten, seemed to have no pests at all. (Interestingly, the wallabies ignored the two unthrifty trees. While insect pests attack a sick tree, birds and mammals are attracted to healthy ones.)

The two unthrifty trees had been planted at the bottom of the orchard. I suspected it was too wet there when I planted them, and I never did get round to pulling them out. They died in the drought, while the trees on the upper (and drier) reaches survived, for by then they had wide and healthy root systems. Even with more soil moisture, the two lower trees did not have the root system or reserves to survive a drought.

Stress kills by making plants more vulnerable to pests and disease. For example, plants can usually cope with temporary waterlogging. However, if pathogens such as *Phytophthora* or fusarium are present, even briefly, lowered oxygen levels can increase root disease. Some plants that seem resistant to infection can be killed by as little as twelve hours of waterlogging. With improved drainage, they may never have shown symptoms at all. (On the other hand, flooding can help control pathogens. Sclerotinia root-rot spores, which can persist in the soil for up to eight years, can be killed by a four-week flooding of the soil.)

CSIRO researchers into eucalypt forests have observed that trees stressed by drought or soil deficiencies were often more susceptible to insect attacks than healthy trees. Trees under stress are more vulnerable and more attractive to pests.

There can be many kinds of stress for plants: growing them in an unsuitable site, damage from animals or machinery (such as lawn mowers), lack of food or lack of moisture. For years a grevillea in my husband's old house grew less healthily than its mates in the row. It and it alone was attacked by woolly aphids. Finally, it began to die back. I investigated. Years ago there had been a slight cut from the lawn mower. Now you could follow dead wood from the old cut down into the roots. It was too late to save it. Perhaps no one even noticed the lawn-mowing accident at the time, or assumed the bush survived it. But slowly the added stress killed the plant.

Other stresses include cold stress. Even if a plant is not burnt by frost it may still become yellowed and drooping due to the cold, and more vulnerable to pest and pathogens, such as salt or herbicide drift, toxins from other plant roots. Heat alone can kill some plants, especially young ones. Two of our first kiwi fruit vines died in the drought, not from dryness, as drip irrigation kept them moist. Simply from the heat, as the temperatures rarely fell below 40°C in the shade. Older vines, with better-established and deeper root systems, were better able to survive.

Wind rock can be a major cause of plant stress, especially in sandy or waterlogged soils or where plants are not yet well established. Hedges and windbreaks stop soil drying out. Wind rock may cause root, limb and leaf damage.

Windbreaks should not be too dense. Thick windbreaks cause turbulence on the other side: wind-born pests are borne downwards, and air currents can damage plants. Make sure some wind can pass through the windbreak. This keeps the currents even, and wind-born pests such as thrips, aphids and pear and cherry slug float overhead.

A windbreak shelters an area up to twenty times its height, but wind direction can change and each area is different.

Controlling pests

Many pests can be controlled simply by knowing their lifecycle and interrupting it. Early apples are less prone to damage from codling moth, early peaches suffer less fruit fly. If you have pasture scarab, ploughing in September to October will break their shells.

Most aphids fly in spring, so early sowings are more vulnerable than late. Late brassicas are less susceptible to grey aphids in mid-summer. Beanfly is more prevalent on early beans. Early corn has fewer helioanthis caterpillars.

Ants will often carry sap-sucking pests, such as aphids, onto plants. Control ants by increasing the amount of organic matter and moisture in your soil (in other words, mulch) or by grease-banding trees to keep them off. Try growing mint around susceptible trees and garden beds.

Other cultural methods of reducing pest numbers include: garden hygiene (prune out infected leaves, pick up fruit, prune out dead wood); crop rotation (removing their hosts will starve many pests); strip harvesting (always leave a strip unharvested for a while to support a residual population of pests and predators).

Encourage mycorrhizas. These are one of the unseen, but important, influences on plant health and plants' ability to cope with disease. Mycorrhizas are symbiotic associations of plant roots and fungi. The fungus either forms a sheath around the root tips of the host or invades the host cells.

The mycorrhizal fungus exudes growth substances, which stimulate young roots to fork so that more nutrients can be absorbed. Phophorus uptake, for example, can triple. The fungal sheath may also release nutrients if needed. Mycorrhizal fungi also produce antibiotics that suppress pathogens such as *Phytophthora* root-rot. Plants with mycorrhizal infections are more disease-resistant.

Encouraging mycorrhizal infections

Specific fungus spores need to be available. Transfer soil from old, diverse gardens with plenty of native species. Mycorrhizas flourish with other soil micro-organisms, soil humus and a decomposing litter layer. Dig as little as possible, mulch, and have as few neat empty spaces in your garden as possible.

Many other soil microflora can help the plant resist pathogens, either by directly attacking the pathogen or dissolving phosphates and other nutrients to increase plant health. Decayed organic materials help to protect plants. For example, potato scurf (which can also affect beans, cabbages and other crops) is suppressed by bacteria and fungi that thrive in decomposing organic matter.

Protecting the garden

- Plant thick scrub and high tree barriers to protect your garden against your neighbours' spray drift, whether pesticide or herbicide, and to keep out pollution from roads.
- Keep up high levels of organic matter in your soil to tie up or break down pollutant residues.
- Convince other people. Small areas of natural pest control are more work and less effective than large ones.

Summary

Pests are a problem only when they are more damage than you can stand. Some pests will never cause damage; others will not build up to dangerous numbers. Know your pests.

Creating a pest problem

- Have a large number of susceptible plants, all the same age, and roughly the same type, without interference from other plants.
- Introduce new pests to your area (such as Mediterranean fruit fly) for which there are few local natural predators.
- Have stressed plants in poor soil, or with too much or too little water, or damaged from stock, heavy pruning, etc.
- Use high-nitrogen fertilisers that promote soft, sappy, disease and pest-prone growth.
- Destroy natural plant communities with the insect and bird predators who live there.
- Use pesticides indiscriminately.

There will be other matters out of your control: weather conditions, for example, with long, cool, wet springs to encourage plagues of aphids; or warm, humid summers with more codling moth eggs, but fewer red spider mite eggs. But if 'unseasonal conditions' keep appearing, they are the normal climate for your area, and you may have to accept you need to grow different plants more suited to your conditions.

Managing pest-prone plants

- Improve the soil with mulch or compost.
- Reduce stress.
- Time your planting better to avoid pests or attract predators or have healthier plants.
- Control ants that may carry sap-sucking and honeydew-producing pests.
- Use deterrent sprays or companion plants. Use pesticides (organic or not) only to give you a breathing space.
- Consider whether the plant is really suited to your area. Dig it out if it is not.
- Use the techniques described to attract predators (p. 20).

COMPANION PLANTING

Companion planting means planting compatible plants in your garden. The trouble is that many people expect too much of companion planting. It is a bit like the myth of true love: introduce carrots to tomatoes and they are supposed to live happily ever after. Companion planting won't cure all your garden problems, although it can help a lot.

Much companion-planting advice is wrong: either untested folklore or, more often, plantings that work in Europe or the USA, but not in Australia. Much of our companion-planting lore is still based on northern hemisphere observations. There is no guarantee that the same benefits will be obtained in Australia, or even in different parts of Australia.

You need to know *why* you are companion planting. A lot of companion-planting advice is of the 'basil like tomatoes' kind. It doesn't tell you why an association works, or how.

Just take one example. It is commonly said that onions planted with carrots will reduce carrot fly. Onions may reduce carrot fly up to 70 per cent, but only if the onions are actively growing. As soon as they stop growing tops and start to bulb, the protective effect is reduced to 30 per cent (that is, when dark night hours are reduced to eight or less). As there are two or more carrot fly flights in a season, you will need more than one onion crop. In addition, there need to be twice as many onions as carrots if they are in alternate rows. However, if the carrots are grown in a block surrounded by several rows of onions, fewer onions are needed.

Several plants are said to be companion crops to brassicas to repel aphids. Aphids recognise brassicas by their silhouette. If other plants are grown among them, the aphids fly on without landing. The companion crop must cover *at least* 50 per cent of the soil area, or it won't be effective. Almost any companion crop will do, as long as it blurs the outlines. But beans or other legumes are best, as they won't reduce the yield and then grow quickly. Slower brassicas can get established before competition from beans.

Suggestions for companion plants in the orchard, vegetable garden, and flower garden are given in chapters 2, 3, and 4 respectively.

How companion planting works

Once you know the principles of companion planting, you can work out associations for yourself. There are four ways that companion planting may help with pest control.

1. Alleopathic association leads to healthier plants. Nettles, for example, 'fix' nitrogen (or their associated bacteria do). Their leaves break down quickly and add humus to the soil; they are reputed

to encourage earthworms and also to transmit some 'tonic' properties to plants not yet specified, but which seem to work. Plants grown with nettles really do seem less prone to pests and diseases and to grow better.

2. Susceptible plants may lure pests to themselves. Chinese cabbage gone to seed, for example, may 'trap' aphids.

3. Plants may deter pests by disrupting the visual and chemical clues that help pests find the host plant.

4. Plants may attract predators.

Guidelines for companion planting

1. Many flowering plants (especially flowering vegetables, such as parsnips and dill, brassicas such as broccoli, native shrubs and buckwheat) attract predators. The adult form of many predators are nectar- or pollen-eaters. And birds, the best predators of all, will be attracted either by the blossoms or the insects around them.

2. Plants with strongly scented foliage may confuse pests.

3. Plants of different shapes may also confuse them. If you are looking for a companion plant for cauliflowers, for example, choose one roughly the same size. A general rule is that the more you interplant, the fewer pests you'll have.

4. Nitrogen-fixing plants will obviously benefit plants near them. It is actually the bacteria associated with their roots that fixes the nitrogen.

5. Deep-rooted plants such as comfrey and chicory will benefit shallow-rooted plants. The deep roots will forage nutrients leached deep down, and as the leaves of the deep-rooters decompose, the nutrients will be made available to the shallow-rooted plants.

6. Some plants release from roots or leaves chemicals that stimulate or suppress the growth of other plants. Sometimes you can tell this from observation.

How to use companion plants

Companion plants may be hedges around your garden (this is especially good for flowering, predator-attracting shrubs). They can be interplanted with other crops, used as paths (for example, chamomile or yarrow), planted under trees, in grassy areas, or even transported in pots. The last is especially good with insect-repelling plants in the vegetable garden: you can ring pest-prone plants with pest-repellents and move them somewhere else when needed. Many aromatic herbs (such as lad's love, tansy and lavender) repel insects such as aphids by 'masking' the crop, but their leaf secretions may also inhibit growth. Large pots will help stop this.

Most companion plants need to be planted ten to twenty days before the pest-prone species.

Examples of companion plants

Plant 'tonics'

Try growing chamomile, lovage, nettles (a nitrogen-fixer and reputed to encourage earthworms), parsley or elder trees. All are reputed to stimulate plant growth in other species. Lupins increase soil nitrogen and are reputed to attract earthworms and increase rose vigour. Foxgloves stimulate other plants around them.

Borage is deep-rooted and brings up leached calcium and potassium. As its leaves decay, these are made available for its companion plants. Borage also attracts bees and a range of pest predators, such as hoverflies. All chamomiles are reputed to add vigour and perfume, revive water-stressed plants and help resistance to pests and diseases. Valerian adds vigour to its companions. It is reputed to make phosphorus more available and to attract earthworms. Yarrow improves the vigour of the plants it grows with, and is reputed to increase the flower perfume and disease resistance.

Nitrogen-fixers

Judas tree, honey locusts, woad, broom (use sterile varieties that won't become a pest), black locust, mesquite, casuarinas, beans, soybean, lucerne, clover, peas, peanuts, lupins, sweet peas, wattles, kennedias, false lucerne tree.

Be careful of: mugwort, sunflowers (these suppress nitrogen-fixing bacteria), most pines, most eucalypts, most cypresses, oak trees, walnuts, pittosporums, lad's love, couch, bracken. They may suppress growth in plants around their drip line.

Weeds

Areas that have more weeds have more predators and other insects. Weeds provide alternative habitats and food supply for predators. Even where they harbour the pests, remember that these are food for predators, and will help ensure that the predators are in your garden when needed.

If you choose to have weeds, you need to control them so that your crop yield is not reduced. This is not as difficult as it seems. Firstly, once a plant is one-third grown, *new* weeds won't reduce the yield. Secondly, the weeds need not be among the crop. They can be in a barrier around or in alternate rows.

Make sure that if you have a good crop of weeds you have other ground covers to replace them in spring. Otherwise, when your annual weeds die, the pests that inhabit them (such as thrips and two-spotted mite) may move to your crops. Alternatively, cut weeds back just before they die, so the pests will have to find alternative hosts *before* they invade your crops.

Control the time weeds flower. Whippersnip off the unopened flower-heads repeatedly until needed. More flower-heads should form. Keep weeds cut back *very* short with a whippersnipper or mower to cut down competition. I find a whippersnipper excellent for slashing weeds in among the vegetables.

Try drip irrigation. Make sure you water only your plants, not the weeds in between. This way the crops will outgrow the weeds, but the stunted weeds will still flower and attract predators.

Weed inhibitors

The following plants will help suppress weeds. Plant them thickly for nuisances such as couch and sorrel: buckwheat, pumpkins, pine needles (these inhibit germination of weeds), poppies, potatoes, rye, oats, walnuts (and any other tree that forms a canopy overhead).

Crops as pest 'traps'

These can be grown to 'trap' pests away from other plants, especially sap-suckers such as aphids: mustard, nasturtiums, Chinese cabbage gone to seed, Chinese mustard.

Plants that attract predators are: flowering native plants, flowering umbellifera, in particular parsnips and dill, brassicas gone to seed, especially broccoli, borage, cornflowers, dill, elder trees, hyssop, lemon and lime balm, honey locust trees, amaranth, day lilies, wallflowers, stocks, ornamental cabbage, forget-me-nots, buddleias.

Plants that repel pests and disease are mostly strongly scented, and thus interfere with the pests' sensing of its target. Some are also insecticidal. Other plants specifically repel certain pests. Most herbs are strongly scented. If you can smell the foliage of a plant when you bend down to it, it will probably interfere with the pests' scenting of their food supply.

Warning. Many strongly aromatic plants contain substances in their leaves that, when washed to the soil by rain or hose, will inhibit the growth of other plants. Although all the trials I have done in my garden haven't shown a marked effect with any of these (in fact many appear to do better) you may prefer to play safe and plant your repellents in pots. These can be taken around the garden whenever you need to protect a crop, and moved during rain or watering.

Please remember that these plants are deterrents, not cures. They will simply make other plants less pleasant to pests, not stop them. If I see a shop that advertises hamburgers, I'll be deterred from going in, but it won't stop me if I'm hungry enough. Repellents are just one part of pest control.

Pest-repellents include: bergamot, castor-oil plant, catnip, cedronella, coreopsis (especially sap-suckers), coriander (aphids and other sap-suckers), clove pinks (while the flowers are blooming), daisy cress (also insecticidal), scented-leaf geraniums or pelargoniums, feverfew (also insecticidal), fleabane, garlic (borers, mites and sap-suckers, but must be regularly trimmed to be effective), horehound, hyssop, Indian beech (seeds are insecticidal, flowers, repel insects), larkspur (aphids, thrips, sometimes grasshoppers and locusts, unless in plague numbers), lavender, pyrethrum (also insecticidal), marigolds (the root secretions also inhibit some nematode species), mustard (the root secretions also repel common problem nematodes), native and introduced pennyroyal, nasturtiums (the leaves are a mild repellent for sap-suckers such as mites, the flowers deter aphids above them), southernwood, rosemary, rue (may also deter dogs, cats, wallabies and rabbits), rhubarb, sacred basil (also insecticidal), stinking roger, sneezeweed (especially ants), tansy, tea tree, several varieties of thistle, tobacco (insecticidal and poisonous, so treat with care), woodruff, wormwood.

The flowers of many of these also attract predators. The effect lasts only while the flowers are blooming.

BIRDS AND OTHER PEST PREDATORS

All living things, including pests, have an essential role to play. Conventional gardeners try to eliminate every pest from their gardens. Natural gardeners see pests as food for predators. Without a food supply you won't have predators in your garden, and when your pest numbers build up (because of seasonal conditions, food supply, weather, etc.) there will be no one to control them, except you.

Fifteen years ago, when I first came to Neverbreak Hills, we had every pest that would survive in the district: year-round fruit fly in the apricots to the oranges; scale, aphids, thrips, two-spotted mite, pear and cherry slug, woolly aphids, codling moth, the list could fill the page. We also had severely depleted soil and trees badly damaged by cattle. For the last six years we haven't had a pest problem. Pests, yes, but they are no longer a problem.

In fourteen years I have learnt to tolerate a little damage. The sight of a few skeletonised cherry tree leaves doesn't chill me any more. A few scale on the lemons no longer worries me. By and large the food produced here compares very favourably with any sold commercially (and our produce was sold through normal commercial channels for several years), though without waxes and artificial colours our produce isn't as glossy or hairless.

Fourteen years ago I panicked at the sight of aphids destroying the new shoots on the citrus trees. Three weeks later, when I had finally bought and assembled spraying equipment, there were no aphids to be seen, but plenty of ladybirds, and their larvae had presumably helped to clean up the problem.

This year, in early spring, there were aphids on the new rose shoots, but not for very long. I watched a yellow robin clean up one rosebush in a morning, while a blue wren attacked the ones under the kitchen window. As I sit here and write this, there are black cockatoos stripping the back off the wattle to get at the borer larvae; there is a rainbow bee-eater, who has decided to ignore the beehives up the hill and dart after cabbage white butterflies instead; a kookaburra is sitting on the swing crunching up a snail, and one of the resident blue wrens is chasing something. I'm not sure what.

These are obvious predators. There are smaller ones, which you will observe only if you watch carefully. This morning I watched a ladybird gradually clean up a scale-infested leaf; a pollistes wasp dropped a paralysed caterpillar in the sink (so I know they are feeding on the cabbage whites in the Brussels sprouts); and another big, orange, ground-dwelling wasp sailed away with another caterpillar as I was picking parsley. There are hoverflies and tiny wasps and lacewings around the flowering parsnips and thryptomene and a dozen other flowers at the moment. I'm not sure what they and their larvae are feeding on, anything from larvae of the codling moth to woolly aphids, but I know that they will be making a large contribution to the pest control in the garden. This year, too, the woolly aphids on the damaged apple trees (some sheep got in and tore them down) are gradually being picked off. The apple tree wounds have healed, and with luck there won't be more woolly aphids. Later in the season there will be some pear and cherry slug, although the wasps and robins and probably others will clear them up.

There are natural controls for all pests, even in the worst inner-city conditions. One female red spider mite, for example, can lay seventy eggs and these can be breeding seven days later. Left unchecked, this means roughly 4 billion red spiders in a month, and roughly two tonnes per acre at the end of the season.

This doesn't happen. Whether you spray or not, other factors will control the mite population: predators, parasites, weather, availability of food, space to live and lay eggs, and natural dispersal.

Attracting predators

No matter how much of an ecological desert your suburb seems, there will be some predators there. Learn to encourage them. This is natural pest control, which is often simply a matter of not jumping in and destroying a working balance. A garden for predators needs the following.

Water

Some predators (such as dragonflies and damsel flies) breed near water, others (such as ichneumon flies) need to drink. Try to create a small, still pond surrounded by plants and moist soil, or even an above-ground birdbath with leafy shrubs around it.

Year-round blossom

The adult forms of many predators feed on blossom, not pests, and blossoms will attract other insects (not necessarily pests), which will also attract insect-eaters. The best blossom is vegetables gone to seed, preferably umbellifera (I let parsnips and dill seed all year round in the garden). The next are native shrubs, as most predators are natives too.

Low pesticide usage

Pesticides, even organic ones, kill predators as well as pests. And without insects to feed on, you won't have predators in your garden.

Other factors

Less digging Many predator eggs and nymphs live in the soil, so the less you disturb the soil, the more predators will survive. Regular ploughing produces dust and helps increase mite and other pest populations. This is because the dust kills small parasites, while not affecting the pests. California red-scale, for example, can be reduced by 50 per cent with a thorough weekly washing of the trees.

Freedom from cats and bees Cats kill lizards, frogs, toads, dragon-flies, mantids, birds and other predators. A large number of bees may compete with hoverflies for nectar.

Honeydew Many adult predators feed on honeydew as well as nectar. Honeydew is the secretion of sap-suckers such as scale and aphids. It is very sweet and can promote sooty mould. If you can tolerate a little sooty mould, do so. Unless it covers more than a quarter of the plant it should do minimal harm and is mostly a cosmetic problem.

Provide nesting boxes These are used in the US in tobacco crops for pollistes wasps as well as birds. The wasps are sheltered from bird and other predators (as well as spray drift) in the boxes.

A yeast-and-sugar solution spray This can help attract lacewings, hoverflies and other sweet-lovers to your garden. A diluted marmite or Vegemite spray is excellent.

Strip harvesting In the USA, lucerne trials showed that strip harvesting (harvesting only one strip at a time) conserved both pests and predators.

Grease-bands Grease-banding on plants where ants are feeding will control them. Ants may transport sap-suckers to plants so they can feed from their sugary secretions. A band of grease at the base of plants will stop this.

Don't burn crop residues This can kill parasitised pests before the parasites can hatch to feed on the pests of the following crop. Let your plant residues break down naturally.

Tolerate some weeds Weeds that attract the pests can act as trap crops as well as a habitat for natural enemies.

Some predators can be gently transferred to where they are needed.

Common predators

Ants

While ants may carry sap-sucking pests onto plants to feed on their sugary secretions, they also feed on many insects, particularly caterpillars, various larvae, fruit fly, codling moth and maggots in the soil. The predatory ant *Myrmecia varians* eats large quantities of lerp psyllids and other small insects.

Some acacias appear to attract ants. The ants get food and shelter from the trees, and the trees are protected from insect attack and competition as the ants clear the ground around the tree. Leave ants alone in the garden. Grease-bands will keep them off plants. Some ants are predatory, and live on other ants on trees.

Assassin bugs

Assassin bugs (not assassin flies) eat beetles, grasshoppers and caterpillars. There are about 240 species so far described in Australia. Most are brown, or reddish-brown to black, some flat and some mantid-like, about 17 mm with or without attractive markings.

Beetles

Soldier beetles and their larvae eat codling moth as well as other larvae and a wide range of sap-suckers and locust and grasshopper and fly eggs. They are up to 18 mm long, with a small, semi-triangular head and long body. They range in colour from yellow through dull orange to bluish black. Soldier beetle eggs are laid on the ground. Plant flowers to attract the adults to feed on flower-dwelling insects.

Calosoma schayeri beetles feed on army worms and cutworms, shredding them in their tough jaws. Tiger beetles and their larvae eat in a wide range of insects, mostly large ones. Some are nocturnal, and will also eat codling moths.

Flower-dwelling beetles range from bright blue to bright yellow. They are mostly carnivorous.

Most of Australia's 300 described *clerid beetles* are pest-eaters, both as adults and larvae, and the larvae in particular are avid predators of wood-boring beetles. They range from about 15 to 40 mm, and some will bite if handled. Many are brightly coloured and patterned. Nectar-producing flowers and water will attract beetles.

Centipedes

Centipedes have only one leg per segment. They eat caterpillars, slugs and other pests. Don't squash them, or confuse them with plant-eating millipedes, which have more than one leg per segment.

Damsel flies

The nymphs and adults consume large quantities of aphids and other sap-suckers. Damsel flies are very similar to dragonflies, though more delicate and slower moving and smaller eyed. They hold their wings erect when resting; dragonflies are kept horizontal. Neither damsel flies or dragonflies sting.

Dragonflies

Dragonflies are excellent mosquito predators, and will catch other insects on the wing, mostly bees, mosquitoes, robber flies, but also butterflies. I have seen them catch cabbage white butterflies and even christmas beetles. They are perhaps the world's fastest insect and can fly at 14 metres per second.

The eggs of both damsel flies and dragonflies are laid either in water, or, in some species, poked into plants growing near water. A pond or dam surrounded by plants may attract dragonflies and damsel flies.

Earwigs

Earwigs mostly feed on detritus. One species feeds on the larvae of codling moth. Damage to seedlings is usually minimal. Earwigs may just happen to be there when something else demolishes them. Damage to buds may be greater. Earwigs can also be a nuisance indoors. See page 84 for control if necessary.

Frogs and toads

These eat insects, slugs, snails. Cats kill frogs and toads. They like moist, leafy shady spots, of which a good garden should have plenty.

Grasshoppers

Long-horned grasshoppers are known as 'katydids' in the USA. There are about 300 species in Australia. Some species eat other insects, though most are vegetarian.

Hoverflies

Hoverflies are perhaps the best predator of all for aphids. They also eat a wide range of scale insects, mites and possibly small larvae, such as pear and cherry slug, and young caterpillars. The many different hoverflies vary substantially in appearance. Some are like small thick bees, others like thin-waisted wasps. They can be recognised by the hovering that gives them their common name, as they dart after pollen and nectar. You'll mostly see them in warm springs and summer.

Hoverfly larvae can eat an aphid a minute, 50 a day, and up to 900 in their lifetime. They actively seek out their prey, range widely and are more active at lower temperatures than other aphid predators, such as ladybirds and their larvae.

Flowering plants attract hoverflies, especially in late winter and spring. Try flowering brassicas. Let cabbages or broccoli go to seed, but cut off the tops just before seeds set, so new flower-heads form. Buckwheat flowers attract hoverflies, also melon and zucchini flowers, flowering sages, flowering dill and parsnips (let them go to seed too, as they will self-sow and you'll always have them), and almost any spring-flowering annual.

Warning to beekeepers. I have noticed bees in late winter and early spring repulsing hoverflies who compete for the same flowers.

Ichneumons

These are neither flies or wasps, although they have been called both. They are parasites, and lay eggs in many pests. They have long, wasp-like eggs and a narrow waist. They are often banded and are mostly around 30-40 mm long.

A common species is *Netelia productus*. These are attracted to light and may come indoors at dusk when the light is on. They are orange to yellow. The females may sting, but it will be less painful than a mosquito sting. They mostly eat caterpillars, including cabbage moth and cabbage white caterpillars and the larvae of codling moth. They will also eat sawfly larvae, including pear and cherry slug.

Lacewings

There are about 400 species of lacewings so far recorded in Australia. Lacewings can be distinguished by their transparent, slightly metallic wings. Both the adults and their larvae eat a wide range of garden pests, including aphids, scale, mealy-bugs, mites, whitefly, thrips, pear and cherry slug, and on at least one occasion I've observed the eating of the larvae of codling moth.

Green lacewing larvae feed only on aphids, and their larvae are sucked dry. One lacewing preys mostly on two-spotted or red spider mite. They also feed on a range of other sap-sucking insects, on butterfly and moth eggs, and the egg capsules of spiders.

Some lacewings lay their eggs on a fine thread or stalk, two or three times as long as the egg. The eggs hatch in about two weeks and the carnivorous larvae live in garden debris on the ground. Ant-lions are the larvae of the ant-lion lacewing. They make deep pits to trap insects.

You can attract lacewings to your garden by mixing marmite or Vegemite and water into a weak-tea-coloured spray, and dousing your plants in it. I've noticed, too, that a range of vegetables going to seed, especially parsnips and radishes, attract lacewings. A garden that is well mulched and not regularly disturbed will mean that more lacewing larvae survive to maturity.

Ladybirds

Both ladybird larvae and many adult ladybirds are pest predators. Ladybird larvae begin to eat scale, aphids, whitefly, mealy-bugs, woolly aphids and other sap-suckers as soon as they hatch. One ladybird larva may eat 100 aphids and several thousand aphoid larvae. Ladybirds have often been introduced in various areas for biological control.

Ladybirds vary in colour from orange and red to blue or green. So far, more than 250 species have been described in Australia. Some are leaf-eaters, most notably the 28-spotted ladybird. If the ladybirds in your garden have 28 spots, they may eat tomato and potato foliage. Otherwise, treasure all ladybirds.

White oil and Bordeaux sprays can wipe out ladybirds, so will derris and pyrethrum sprays. Try rhubarb spray instead. If you are prone to scale infestations on new growth in spring, and spray your trees with Bordeaux or oil sprays in winter, you may find your problem solved if you spray only every second tree, wait ten days, then spray the rest. This way you keep a residual ladybird population that can still build up for spring.

Lizards

These eat slugs, snails, flies and other insects, depending on the type of lizard. Protect them from cats, give them rocky places to shelter in or a good thick bush garden.

Parasites

There are a wide range of parasites for all insect pests. While these usually don't kill the pest, they make them vulnerable to predators by making them slower. There is very little you can do to increase parasitism of your pests, with a few exceptions mentioned through the text, so I won't detail parasite infections here.

Praying mantids

Australia has over a hundred species of praying mantids. The most common are green and brown. You can distinguish these from locusts by their 'praying' position, with their strong forelegs lifted up. Young mantids eat aphids, leafhoppers. Old mantids eat the larger caterpillars, bugs, beetles and sometimes moths and other insects. Mantids tend to stay put if they have enough food, as long as you don't have a mantid-catching cat to scare or eat them. Mantids are active during both night and day, although their green and brown colour camouflages them well.

Mantid eggs are laid in a frothy mass attached to a surface such as a tree or fence. Look out for them, and don't disturb them. Alternatively, keep them in an open jar indoors so they aren't parasitised by wasps. They take from four to six months to hatch. Separate them at once, so they don't eat each other. Even though mantids are carnivorous they can be raised on raw apple, potato and other raw fruit, live or dead insects, and crumbs of meat. Use a netted fish tank, with only one mantid at a time in each. They can turn cannibal.

Robber or assassin flies

These eat any insect they can catch, mostly flying insects. They will also impale human fingers if you try and catch them. They are long, thin flies, hairy, with thick legs. Their wing spans can range from 2 to 75 mm. The larvae are cyclindrical grubs living in soil or old timber.

Scorpion flies

The many scorpion flies in Australia vary considerably in appearance. They can resemble lacewings or cockroaches. They all have long, spindly legs and long, transparent wings, with opaque veins. The wings are held over the abdomen like a tent when they are resting. None has the raised tip of the abdomen that gives scorpion flies their name: these are found only overseas.

Scorpion flies need damp places or water. They prey on flies, bees, caterpillars and beetle larvae. They pupate just below the soil. Only the males are predatory, securing insects to feed the females during mating. The females feed on nectar.

Nectar-producing plants will attract scorpion flies. Also damp or marshy places, preferably with water, and undisturbed soil for pupating.

Spiders

Spiders live almost entirely on insects, and certainly not just web-caught flies and mosquitoes. They will eat caterpillars, including the larvae of codling moth, flying termites, butterflies, whiteflies.

Stilt flies

These are small flies with a wing span of up to 15 mm. They are thin and tapering, green to brown, with long thin legs. They will feed on aphids. Damp and wet places, plenty of foliage will attract stilt flies.

Tachinid flies

Tachinid flies pollinate plants as well as predate pests. Their larvae are parasitic in the bodies of beetles and moths. The adults resemble thick-bodied, bristly blowflies, some much smaller and some much larger than house flies. They eat a wide range of pests. Don't kill flies unless you are sure they're houseflies or common blowflies.

Wasps

There are many species of wasps that either predate or parasitise pests. They eat a wide range of caterpillars, including those of the cabbage white butterfly, pear and cherry slug, and codling moth. Not all wasps sting, so don't automatically reach for the aerosol if they are around the house. Some wasps also attack scale and parasitise the eggs of a range of pests. *Chalcid wasps* (metallic blue/black/brown and about 1 mm long) parasitise beetles and mealy-bugs, as well as a range of eggs, scale and caterpillars. The flower wasps are excellent parasitisers of scarab beetle larvae and many other moth larvae.

Ground wasps dig burrows in the sand. The most common is the large orange and black wasp, which grows up to 35 mm long. I have watched them carry away enormous quantities of cabbage white caterpillars as well as pear and cherry slug, although they attacked the latter only when they were numerous. Having accidentally sat on one, I can say that while not at all aggressive; they do sting, but not too severely.

Flower wasps are mostly large, hairy and bright blue. They are excellent predators of scarab beetles. A wide range of flowers through the year will attract flower wasps.

Some *paper wasps* are common wasps, with thin-combed nests hung from a slender stalk. Others are rarer. All build their nests out of chewed wood 'paper'. Some will give a painful sting, but they aren't aggressive. We have large numbers of two sorts around the house, and even with extreme provocation they have never bitten anyone. They eat caterpillars, spiders, pear and cherry slug, aphids, in fact whatever seems to be the most numerous at the time.

Mud wasps build clay nests, often on the walls of buildings. They grow up to 30 mm long and have conspicuously slender waists. One of the most common is orange with a black band (not to be confused with the European wasp). Mud wasps predate caterpillars, spiders and possibly other pests.

Club or *cicada hunter sphecid wasps* eat a wide range of pests. The 420 species so far described in Australia may eat caterpillars, locusts, beetles, spiders and other insects, depending on the size of the wasps and the prey.

Attracting birds

Birds are the most adaptable pest predator of all. Unlike most insect predators they move from one food supply to another, depending on its abundance. Birds will often take up to 40 per cent of a pest on a plant. I have watched yellow robins completely clearing aphids off a rose, kookaburras gulping snails all morning, blue wrens guzzling caterpillars, bee-eaters snapping cabbage white butterflies.

There is a time lag, however. When I first came here there were no snails. Gradually I brought them in, accidentally, in pots from nurseries. At first the snails were a real problem. It took about three years of abundant snails for the kookaburras to discover them. Now the snails are kept under control.

Don't expect to have your pest problems solved as soon as you begin to attract birds to your garden. But even if they never caught a pest at all, you would still have the glory of the birds to comfort you.

Water

Nearly all birds need water (some survive on flower nectar), and free-standing water is usually in short supply in many suburbs. Some birds, such as willy wagtails, also like to nest near water. Water also attracts many insects: more food for birds.

Preferably, water should be deep enough so birds can bathe. Make sure there is a place for the birds to perch, so they can drink. Even small containers of water will supply many birds. They have 'pecking orders' and will drink one after another. All water should be out of the reach of cats. Water also needs to be fresh. Think about a dripper attached to some half-inch black plastic pipe, continually refreshing the birdbath or pond.

One way of making a simple cat-proof drinker is to suspend a container of water on a rope, say an icecream container with the lid glued around it as a perch. Bigger birdbaths should have sloping sides or a rock in the middle so birds can bathe there as well as drink. Leptospermum or other shrubs may be placed near birdbaths (unless there are cats near by). They provide good perching places.

Ponds should have a boulder or other drinking place at least a metre from the sides, where cats can't leap onto them. Let ponds slope gently, with boggy reedy areas at the edges, again to attract insects as well as water birds.

Broken light is best for birdbaths. The water is kept relatively cool and the semi-shade may give small birds a feeling of security.

Shelter

Small birds need shelter from larger birds, cats, dogs, etc. Plant shrubs close together to form thickets. Try prickly plants, such as grevilleas and hakeas. Use native grasses and grass-like plants to encourage nesting. Make sure you have 'landing' trees too. Dead or leafless or open-branched trees such as eucalypts are excellent.

Birds like to perch. Some birds (owls and kookaburras, for example) need high lookouts, such as a pergola or the branch of a gum tree. Some like low, prickly, protected bushes. Provide a variety.

Nesting

Birds may nest in tree hollows, mud banks, grass, reeds, prickly shrubs, etc. Tree hollows and prickly shrubs are the two most common nesting places. If you don't have tree hollows, make one. Hollow out a piece of wood and tie it to a branch. Hollow crevices can be made the same way. Forget about bird houses. Birds don't live in houses, though some do like their eaves.

Pesticides

Many pesticides are cumulative. They are passed on up the food chain. Birds may be affected by pesticide-killed insects, or by infected water. They may then be killed in their turn or rendered infertile, or simply be driven elsewhere for lack of food.

Food

This must be regular or supplemented. Make sure you have flowers, seeds, fruit or whatever your bird population needs all the year round. This is best achieved by a constant succession of flowering shrubs, which will fruit and seed in turn.

Nectar-producing plants will not only feed the nectar-eaters, but attract insects for the insect-eating ones for the times when there are no large pest numbers on your plants. Many nectar-eating birds eat insects during nesting, or when there is a plague of insects, a possibly irresistible source of easy food. (In addition, many adult predators such as wasps and hoverflies feed on nectar. Flowering plants will attract them and predators such as tachinid flies.)

Cats

If you own a cat please don't attract birds to your garden. *Every cat catches birds.* Some, however, have learnt to do it discreetly. If you have neighbouring cats (and most people do), either fence them out with overhanging wire or spray them with the hose whenever you see them in your garden. While dogs may chase birds, they can't climb, and a dog may keep your garden cat-free. Many birds are also fond of dog food.

I love cats. But cats eat lizards, frogs and other predators as well as birds. They are simply not compatible with a natural Australian garden. If you do have an indispensable cat (say an aged friend of the family):

• Feed it regular, small meals so it never hunts from hunger.
• Discourage it from catching birds with whatever punishment you usually give it (disapproval may be enough).
• Try to train it to seek amusement from toys, dangling wool, etc. Most cats hunt for interest, not food.
• Try covering dead decoy birds with chilli paste.

Pests and their predators

These are just a few of the possible predators for your pests, drawn either from my own observation or from the observation of people I trust. No more than a fraction of the world's insects have been identified, much less have had their eating habits studied. Some predators eat different food in different circumstances. Some predators are probably limited to very small areas. This list is simply a guide, an indication of the incredible diversity of creatures that may be involved in controlling your pests, and which you can attract to your garden.

Pest	Predator
Aphids	*Birds* Wrens (prefer low branches or tussocks to nest in), silvereyes, firetails, willy wagtails (like to nest near water), grey shrike thrush, sparrows (some), eastern spinebills (sometimes), finches (some during nesting), yellow and other robins, honey-eaters, thornbills, kingfishers (sometimes), tree creepers, cuckoo shrike, wrens, pardalotes, and whistlers. *Other predators* Ladybird larvae, lacewings (especially the green lacewing), hoverflies, damsel bugs, stilt flies, paper wasps, mantids, ants, and various wasps.
Beanfly	Damsel bugs, hoverflies, lacewings, ladybirds and their larvae, mantids, stilt flies, ants, and various wasps.
Beetles	Assassin bugs, various wasps, dragonflies, mantids, scorpion flies, and tachinid flies.

Pest	Predator
Borers	*Birds* Black cockatoos, sitellas, tree creepers, and currawongs.
	Other predators Clerid beetles, scorpion flies (eat larvae), dragonflies, sphecid, chalcid and flower wasps, tachinid flies, assassin bugs, ants, spiders, earwigs.
Bugs	Mantids, dragonflies, robber or assassin flies.
Cabbage white butterfly caterpillars	Assassin bugs, mantids, centipedes, dragonflies, hoverflies eat small caterpillars, ichneumons, lacewings (eat the eggs), scorpion flies, spiders, and various wasps.
Caterpillars	*Birds* Cuckoos (eat hairy caterpillars too), rosellas, noisy miner, Richard's pippit, trillers, rufous whistler, shrike thrush, flycatcher, monarchs, cicada bird, pardalotes, magpies, choughs, magpie larks, currawongs, grey shrike thrush, starlings (sometimes), and yellow robins.
	Other predators Scorpion flies, spiders, tachinid flies, chalcid, flower, paper and other wasps, ichneumons, centipedes, ants, assassin bugs, dragonflies (eat butterflies and moths), hoverflies, lacewings, scorpion flies.
Christmas beetles	Assassin bugs, various wasps, dragonflies, mantids, scorpion flies, tachinid flies.
Codling moths	*Birds* Owls, night jars, and swifts.
	Other predators Lacewings and their larvae, spiders, tachinid flies, chalcid wasps (eat the eggs), flower, paper and other wasps, earwig (at least one species eat the larvae), tiger and other beetles, mantids, ants, and ichneumons. Many caterpillar-eaters eat the larvae stage of codling moth.
Cutworms	Calosoma beetles and tiger beetles, ants, spiders, and various soil dwelling larvae.
Fruit flies	Ants, predatory flies may catch them on the wing; predators may have a very small role in controlling introduced fruit fly.
Grasshoppers	*Birds* Bustards, straw-necked ibis, fantails, willy wagtails, cuckoos, owls, kingfishers, noisy friar birds, Richard's pippit, scarlet and yellow robins, chooks (these must be free-range chooks used to vigorously hunting their food), and honey-eaters.
	Other predators Soldier beetles, assassin bugs, and sphecid wasps.
Lerps	*Birds* Honey-eaters, cuckoo shrikes, firetails, blue wrens, and some finches during nesting.

Pest	Predator
Lerps *(cont.)*	*Other predators* Predator ants, various wasps, possibly lacewing larvae.
Mites	Damsel bugs, hoverflies, lacewings, ladybirds and their larvae, mantids, stilt flies, ants, and various wasps.
Pear and cherry slug	*Birds* Cuckoo shrikes, scarlet and yellow robins, silvereyes, currawongs, thornbills (sometimes), and firetails. *Other predators* Lacewings, ichneumons, paper wasps, probably various other wasps.
Sawflies	Hoverflies, ichneumons, pollistes and other wasps, spiders, lacewings (eat the eggs).
Scale	*Birds* Tree creepers, cuckoo shrikes, pardalotes, silvereyes, firetails, honey-eaters, blue wrens, and finches (some during nesting). *Other predators* Ladybirds and their larvae, lacewings, hoverflies, chalcid wasps, damsel bugs, mantids, stilt flies, ants, various wasps.
Snails	*Birds* Kookaburras, currawongs, magpies (sometimes), owls (sometimes), pittas, trillers (sometimes), mynahs (sometimes), night jars, butcher birds, glossy ibis, chooks, and ducks. *Other predators* Lizards, centipedes, various beetles (especially snail eggs), frogs, toads.
Thrips	*Birds* Tree creepers, Richard's pippit, cuckoo shrike, pardalotes, firetails, honey-eaters, blue wren, thornbill, whistlers, shrike thrush, and wood swallows (sometimes, as they dip for nectar). *Other predators* Ladybird larvae, lacewings and their larvae, damsel bugs, and spiders.

CHAPTER 2

The Pest-free Orchard

General rules

- Avoid planting all one species, all deciduous or evergreen, or all one age. This just gives pests a smorgasbord. Interplant with flowering shrubs and nitrogen-fixers.
- Don't plant trees where a similar one has been. Trees can be poisoned by the root residues of old ones, or the soil may be depleted, or there may be levels of pathogens that the old tree gradually got used to, but the new one can't tolerate.
- Feed trees with mulch and other decomposing organic matter. Ignore the temptation to 'fast feed', although in some cases a temporary, homemade, liquid foliar spray can be used. High-nitrogen feeding (especially in spring) can lead to pest attacks.
- Remove old stumps of gums and wattle that may host spores of wood or root-rotting fungi.
- Plants need water to carry their nutrients. Make sure plants have enough: not a once-a-week splurge, but drip irrigation if possible, and mulch. Continual damp soil is better than alternating wet and dry.
- Prune as little as possible, and only to encourage new wood (if necessary) for fruit production. The more you cut the tree, the more you need to feed it, and the more soft, sappy pest-prone new growth will develop. Pruning cuts may also let in wood-rotting fungi and other pathogens or encourage woolly aphids. Open trees are more prone to bird damage.
- Recycle. Even prunings decompose. Old fruit can be sealed in a plastic bag until it rots, killing possible fruit fly, codling moth and other pests into the bargain.
- Maximise leaf cover, for weed and moisture control and soil

protection, but remember that trees need a good air flow and that over-shaded trees may be prone to some pests and pathogens. Strike a balance. Orient your trees so they catch the morning sun.

• Don't dig. Mulch and mow. Leaf mulch and litter give predators such as beetles and ground-digging wasps more food and shelter from climatic extremes and disturbance. Lucerne hay, sewage sludge and leaf mould help to inhibit nematodes in the soil. Dust on the leaves may kill predators and encourage pests such as red spider mites.

Orchard hygiene is the best orchard pest control. Pick up any fallen fruit at once or, better still, let animals scavenge it. Remove all dried fruit mummies every winter, pick off diseased leaves and fruit as they appear. Inspect your fruit for codling moth or fruit fly damage; pick them off and let them decompose in a sealed plastic bag.

Never leave fallen fruit on the ground.

Companion plants for the orchard

The following plants are excellent companions in the orchard, although the companion plants mentioned in chapter 1 are, of course, effective here as well, especially the general pest repellents and predator attractors.

Pasture under trees

Grass is not necessarily the best ground cover for orchards. Couch grass, for example, releases a growth inhibitor from its roots, and this stunts the roots of several fruit trees. Kikuyu may choke trees and compete for nutrients and moisture. If you do choose to have grass under your trees, try mixing several other species to make an orchard ley.

Lucerne is an excellent crop to grow below fruit trees, as long as it is mown very short. Mown lucerne responds in the same way as grass by forming a sward. It is perennial, nitrogen-fixing, and is reputed to encourage earthworms. The roots will continue to travel down year after year: I have known them to go 7 metres down a rocky well site. Once lucerne roots are deep enough, they will no longer compete with your fruit trees, and the deep roots will bring up leached nutrients, which will become available to your plants as the lucerne is mown and the tops break down.

Any grass should be mixed with nitrogen-fixing clover, the sort of clover will depend on your district. Subterranean clovers will also help add organic matter to your soil, as will any mown orchard sward.

Don't grow buttercups or other ranunculi or sunflowers in clover. They inhibit it.

All legumes are said to be stimulated by a small proportion (up to 10 per cent) of mustard in the mix. Mustard is quick-growing annual, readily reseeding.

Think about planting flowers under your trees. Dandelions produce ethylene, which will induce your flowers and fruiting trees to bloom earlier, though the flowers may not last as long. This effect will be related to how windy your garden is: a still, warm garden will mean a greater effect from the ethylene. Dandelions are also deep rooted, and will bring up nutrients leached deep down, returning them to the soil as the dandelion leaves decompose. Dandelions are also reputed to encourage earthworms and improve soil condition.

Nettles increase nitrogen-fixing bacteria and improve the quality of the soil, although they are perhaps not the best orchard companions. Pricking can be a problem with bare legs.

Our neighbours grow nasturtiums under their fruit trees. Nasturtiums repel aphids and other sap-suckers flying *above* them. They are also a good ground cover, not exhausting the soil or demanding too much moisture, and keeping moisture in as well as weeds out. The only drawback with nasturtiums is that they are annual in cold areas and frost kills them, so you are left with bare soil. An alternative is to plant the nasturtiums every year when you mulch the trees, along with some mustard seeds perhaps. The mulch will have broken down by the time frosts arrive and your other orchard species will take over the bare ground.

Plants to attract predators

I rely on flowering parsnips, which are regularly mown, flower again and seed themselves. Parsnips are hard to grow only when the seed is old. Fresh seed will germinate anywhere.

Other flowering herbs that may attract predators include fennel, carraway, dill, hyssop and lemon and lime balm. Flowers grown under fruit trees, including bulbs such as daffodils, especially the highly scented ones, seem to attract insects and bird predators.

Plants to discourage pests

Chives under apple trees are reputed to inhibit scab, although the chives must be regularly cut or grazed to be effective. Nasturtiums inhibit aphids and woolly aphids.

Garlic planted under fruit trees is reputed to help control leaf diseases such as leaf spot and curly leaf. Again, it must be regularly cut to be effective. Garlic around trees and shrubs is reputed to repel borers, mites and weevils if the tops are regularly picked.

Rosemary, coriander, nettle, spearmint and chives are reputed to repel aphids and woolly aphids. Flowering parsnips help repel codling moth, possibly by attracting predator wasps and hoverflies.

Catnip and tansy are said to repel ants that may carry sap-sucking pests such as aphids. The ants feed on their sugary secretions and may transmit viruses. I have never found either effective, and rely on grease-banding instead. Crotaria helps control eelworms; mustard a range of nematodes.

Strawberries grown under peaches may increase the number of parasites that control the oriental fruit moth. Blackberries around vineyards appear to reduce the numbers of grapeleaf hoppers by increasing alternative hosts for parasitic wasps.

An abundance of various weeds appears to reduce the number of San José scale and tent caterpillar on apple trees, aphids and cabbage white butterfly caterpillars on Brussels sprouts, beanfly on mung beans, stinkbugs on soybeans. Weed cover needs to be manipulated so it doesn't interfere with cropping while still providing diversity.

Major fruit pests

The more you know about a pest the better able you are to devise a management strategy to avoid problems with it. For all pest problems, remember that healthy, unstressed trees in good, humus rich soil are less prone to pest damage. Concentrate on growing your plants, not killing the pests. Bother about pest damage only when the problem can't be ignored.

Aphids

There are few cultivated plants that at some time aren't attacked by aphids. Aphids are sap-suckers, clustering on new, sappy growth, just as it is most vulnerable to attack, reducing the quantity and quality of the crop, even restricting the growth of the entire plant, especially if water is scarce. Plants may also become stunted due to leaf and shoot distortion.

Aphids can transmit viruses. Even where aphid numbers aren't enough to cause damage themselves, their potential as virus carriers may necessitate their control. Plants are at their most susceptible to virus when they are producing new growth, the time when plants are also most vulnerable to aphid attack. Sooty mould can also be caused by aphids, from the sweet honeydew they excrete.

Most aphids in Australia are introduced pests that feed on introduced species. Of about 135 species of aphids in Australia, only about 50 are native. Their appearance varies considerably, sometimes depending on what they are feeding on. Many aphids are parthenogenetic females: they don't need males to reproduce. The different species of aphid attack different food and ornamental plants. One of the most damaging aphid is the root-sucking phylloxera, which wiped out several wine industries over the years. Phylloxera-resistant root-stock is recommended for vineyards.

Aphids are also known as 'ant cows'. Their sweet honeydew secretion is gathered by ants (and bees and the adult forms of various predators too). Several species of ants may gather aphid eggs, taking them to their underground nests during winter. When they are about to hatch, the ants carry eggs back to the roots of the plants on which they will feed. In exposed feeding grounds ants may protect them from ant-lions and ladybirds, or build them shelters, carry them off to new food areas.

Control of aphids

Try deterrents, companion planting, and encouraging predators. The most effective pest control often involves a managing your crop so that pests don't become a problem. With aphids this may be as simple as changing your sowing times.

The green peach aphid is a pest of young fruit trees, distorting young foliage. It also may carry the virus potato leaf roll as well as cucumber mosiac. The green peach aphid can be yellow-brown or green. Plants sown in late summer or autumn are less susceptible to the green peach aphid.

The grey cabbage aphid is most active in early to late spring. If you need to protect your brassica crop from the grey cabbage aphid, don't plant seedlings till December. And try to avoid sudden growth flushes from intermittent irrigation and fertilisation.

Late sowings (November, January) should cut down infestation of the carrot aphid.

Another management technique involves planting *Casuarina stricta* breaks. Aphids are often blown by the wind from warmer areas, and are unable to feed on casuarina windbreaks.

Predators

While aphids have a large number of predators, especially birds, ladybirds and their larvae, hoverflies, etc., the early spring infestation of aphids usually occurs before predator numbers can build up to cope with them.

Aphid numbers build up quickly in early spring in response to the warmer weather. While there may be other population peaks at subsequent growth flushes during the growing season, especially in autumn, it is this spring build up that is often the most troublesome, as predators such as ladybirds and lacewings probably will not control them until summer. The blue-green aphid, for example, can tolerate temperatures as low as 2.5°C, where as lacewings need 6°C and the 11-spotted ladybird 10°C.

Aphid populations continue to build up as the weather gets warmer. In early spring it may take fifteen days from one generation to another; but in late spring it may only take a week. As aphid densities increase, the reproductive rate appears to slow down, although in some species aphids simply migrate. With rose aphids there may be other 'flushes' matching the growing flushes and budding of the roses.

Aphid numbers also build up in autumn, but this is less consistent than the spring build up, which is almost entirely dependent on temperature. The autumn build up can be affected by predators, food supply, etc. Unfortunately most predators have most influence on aphids after they reach their population peak, not while numbers are increasing. The major exception to this is birds.

Birds   In our area, at least, birds are the most consistent aphid predator. If you encourage a resident population of small birds, you will have a ready aphid control at any time of the year. Even many nectar-eaters will attack aphids and other insects in spring, the time of the worst aphid infestation. I have seen one male blue wren clean up three rosebushes of aphids in an afternoon. A flock of silvereyes will provide control for a paddock of cauliflowers.

Like any other predator, birds need a year-round food supply:

flowering plants for insects and nectar, seeding grasses, as well as protected nesting places and water sources.

Spiders are also an effective aphid predator, and are less vulnerable than birds to the residual effects of pesticides.

Entomophthora   A fungal disease, *Entomophthora* also attacks aphids in warm, humid weather. Infected aphids turn orange. If orange aphids are noticed, try spreading the disease by stickytaping twigs with infected aphids onto other areas.

Hoverflies   Hoverflies, like ladybirds, are valuable predators later in summer when the larval numbers build up. Adult hoverflies need nectar-producing flowers.

Lacewings   These are a more effective aphid predator. They are active throughout the year. Pine windbreaks are said to encourage early lacewing build up, as do flowering plants, especially winter-flowering native species. Lacewings are also attracted by sprays of marmite or yeast.

Ladybirds   Ladybirds are often regarded as a major aphid predator, possibly because ladybirds are highly coloured and visible. Unfortunately ladybirds play only a small role in keeping down the worst of aphid numbers, especially in spring. Ladybird predation is more important in mid-summer. Eggs are laid in the litter around plants, and the larvae live on aphids dropping off to the ground. Only later do the ladybirds move up the plant. Ladybirds also have a summer resting-stage, with little predation. Ladybirds need 'resting-sites' for overwintering: old wood such as fence posts and logs, old flower pots and, especially, conifers.

Parasites   There are many small parasites of aphids, including parasitic small wasps. These insert their eggs into the aphid body, and the larvae then eat the aphid. If you see brown aphid 'mummies' attached to plants, they have probably been parasitised. Many adult parasitic wasps also need nectar-producing flowers.

Control of sappy growth

Aphids are usually 'flush' feeders, preferring young tips, buds and shoots. Numbers are mostly dependent on the availability of food. If you cut down the amount of new, sappy growth your plants produce, you will greatly cut down the infestation of aphids to a level available predators can cope with. This does not mean stopping the growth of your plants, simply trying to space it more evenly throughout the growing season, instead of a succulent burst in spring.

Any efficient organic fertilising regime will help with this. Avoid high-nitrogen fertilisers, relying instead on the steady release of nutrients from decaying organic matter in the soil. Don't use any fertiliser in late winter when there will be excess nitrogen free in spring. Don't water once a week, or when the soil is dry. Constant moisture from drip irrigation and mulch is more effective, and not only in controlling aphids.

It is no myth that organically grown produce has a greater resistance to many pests, including aphids. If you doubt this, organise your own trials. Feed one lot of plants with urea and another, across the garden or orchard, with compost. Note the level of pest infestation on each.

Traps

Aphids can be trapped. Try scattering yellow-painted boards through your growing area, liberally painted with glue or any other sticky substance. A large number of aphids should be caught. An easier trap involves yellow pans of shallow water. The aphids are attracted by the colour, and drown. A little oil can be added to discourage mosquitoes and make the trap more effective.

Repellents

One of the most effective aphid repellents is reflective mulch. This can be bought commercially, or any reflective substance can be used. There is no need to keep it down all the time, only during growing spurts when plants are vulnerable.

Other repellents include barriers of strong herbs, especially rhubarb and marigolds. Aphids are inhibited by nasturtiums *underneath* them, a useful companion plant in the orchard, where nasturtiums can ramble under trees, but less so in vegetable areas where the nasturtiums may be higher than the plants.

If aphids are being carried onto your plants by ants, grease-banding should prevent them.

Encouraging aphids

Several techniques are almost infallable for attracting aphids. They include:
• Bordeaux and oil spraying in winter. These will kill overwintering predators. Never spray all your trees with Bordeaux at one time.

Closely packed cabbages show signs of caterpillar damage; cabbages interplanted with other crops would show less damage.

Leaf-eating larvae of the citrus butterfly. Use Dipel, flour or derris, and encourage birds, wasps, and other predators.

Webbed leaves can be a symptom of leaf-eating ladybirds, red spider mite, some caterpillars, or sawfly larvae; but all are killed by derris dust: you don't always have to know precisely what pest harms your plant to be able to decide on a strategy.

Brown rot on a nectarine: use Bordeaux in winter, clean up old fruit "mummies" and prune off dead wood; use seaweed and chamomile spray in summer. Hot water can cut down post-harvest brown rot.

A fruit fly infected tomato: use traps, repellent, and stringent garden hygiene to clean up all ripe and fallen fruit and vegetables.

Two-spined citrus bugs. Clean up fallen fruit that may attract them; try scented geraniums under the trees; if necessary, use a pyrethrum or derris spray.

Spray half, wait two weeks, then spray the rest, so that a remnant of pests and predators will survive.
- High nitrogenous growth in poor soil. This promotes soft, sappy, aphid-attracting growth.
- Monocultures. Plants of the same variety, age and susceptibility are more likely to suffer severely from pests, with less reprieve from predators. Predators need a constant food supply, which a one-crop situation won't give them.

Organic pesticides

These may be necessary to prevent virus spread by even small numbers of aphids, or because of seasonal conditions. The worst time for aphids is when spring is long and slow, usually rainy days, so the plants produce lots of sappy growth, but the temperature hovers around 10°C: warm enough for aphids, too cold for most of their predators. Try insect-repellent sprays of red pepper, mustard, lavender, rosemary, wormwood. If these fail, try clay spray (but be careful not to spray on predators such as ladybirds and their larvae), glue spray, oil sprays if the temperature is below 24°C, bug juice, nettle spray, wormwood, turnip or parsnip spray for pea aphids, onion, lantana, garlic spray, pyrethrum, feverfew, rhubarb sprays. Use the last three only if the others fail.

Codling moth

We expect all our fruit, including apples, to be blemish free. A wormy apple is a joke, to be avoided. Over the past forty years the chemicals sprayed in apple orchards have become stronger and more dangerous, all to produce the perfect apples we expect, while the pesticide resistance of codling moth continues to grow.

There are two ways to go about achieving organic codling moth control. The first needs several years work to achieve, wiping out all codling moth from your orchard. It is a lot of work and needs vigilance after that. Luckily, however, codling moth don't move very far, and once you have got a 'clean' growing area, it should remain so as long as your orchard hygiene is maintained. As a minor recompense, you should have less trouble with other pests, such as light-brown apple-moth and scale, as natural predators build up to control them.

The second way is to rely on natural predators and good orchard hygiene to keep the numbers of codling moth under reasonable control. I know we have codling moth, the trees used to be severely infested and the odd apple is wormy even now. But changes in our growing regime have kept the infestation to acceptable levels.

Codling moths are an introduced pest, now spread worldwide. They originated in Europe and gained their common name from the wild codling tree from which modern varieties of apples are derived. They have no native food sources, only orchard ones— apples, and to a lesser extent pears, hawthorn fruit, walnuts, quinces, peaches, nectarines and plums—as well as an occasional eggplant.

Even with these alternative sources near by, the codling moths will probably stick to your apple trees. If they are proving hard to eradicate, you may also need to look at other sources of infection.

Codling moths are about 20 mm from wing tip to wing tip, greyish-brown, with a circular, slightly dark, shiny area near each wing tip. They lay their eggs on or near the fruit when the temperature is 15°C or more. The eggs look like tiny, flat, circular scales. They hatch in one or two weeks, depending on temperature, and the young caterpillar enters the fruit, usually from the top or bottom, and chews its way down into it.

This is the part of the caterpillar's life that causes the damage, and when it is the hardest to control. The caterpillar may eat the seeds causing the fruit to drop, the apple may rot, or a late infection may mean the caterpillar is still there when the fruit is consumed.

When feeding is completed, after three to five weeks, the caterpillars commonly shelter either on the butts of trees or in wooden objects next to the tree, such as old ladders and fruit boxes and corners of sheds. There they spin a cocoon. They usually emerge in spring, although there can be several hatchings a year, and they can also remain dormant up to two years. The peak time of adult activity is October to December, with another hatching in December to January. Usually in cool areas, such as Tasmania, there is only one generation a year, and control is easier. There may be up to three generations in warmer areas. This makes control of long-maturing apples such as Granny Smith particularly difficult.

Adults shelter in the foliage during the day and become active at dusk and just before dawn. They won't mate until the temperature is over 12-15°C. Eggs are rarely laid more than 50 metres from the females' cocoon, and males rarely travel more than 100-200 metres.

In a 1975 CSIRO experiment in Victoria, thirty-six apple trees were placed in wire cages from which moths could neither escape nor enter. In spite of exhaustive searches and two sprayings of ryania it wasn't until 1977 that the pest was wiped out in the enclosures.

Once codling moth has been wiped out in your orchard, however, you have a good chance of keeping it under control. If you can eliminate codling moth in the area around you, and stop reinfestation from infested boxes, etc., chances of a large-scale reinfestation are slight.

Once it is inside the apple, control of the codling moth organically is difficult. You need to rely on controlling the moths and caterpillars before they get to the apples by rigorous orchard hygiene.

Orchard hygiene

As soon as apples form, they must be checked every ten days for holes in the top and bottom. Caterpillars feed for three to five weeks on apples before they pupate, sometimes in more than one apple. As they feed, more detritus gets pushed out of the hole: this is what you are looking for. All infected apples must be removed and burnt or fed to animals, not buried or composted. If possible, keep animals running under the trees (chooks, sheep, pigs, wombats) who will eat any fallen apples. These are likely to be infected, as any damage to the seeds may cause the apple to fall.

Remove all old boxes and ladders from the orchard. Don't bring in second-hand ones unless you check them carefully for cocoons. Check corners of sheds regularly too. Check flowering trees and crabapples, and quinces and any apples in storage for signs of rotting; they may also be infected. Remember, any moth that escapes means a thousand more at the end of the season.

Note: Many people mistake fruit fly damage for codling moth. If you have large black-brown soggy areas in your fruit—possibly with many small 'grubs' still feeding—you have fruit fly.

Natural predators

Natural predation may be enough to control codling moth sufficiently for home consumption, as long as you make sure all fallen fruit is picked up or eaten by stock as soon as it falls. Encourage natural predators with flowering plants, especially umbellifera, such as flowering parsnips, and water. (See also pp. 48 and 22-33.)

Many birds eat codling moth caterpillars, although the amount of control they provide is limited, as the pests soon disappear into the apple. Owls, swifts and other birds take a larger toll of the moths at night, as do spiders and ants. At least one species of earwig feeds mostly on codling moth larvae, usually when they are looking for a place to hibernate. Ants also attack them at this time.

A possibly greater source of control is the tiny parasitic *Trichogramma* wasp. These may destroy up to 30 per cent of autumn-laid eggs. Mirid bugs also kill a number of larvae.

Once the larvae are hibernating, up to 50 per cent can be killed by the larvae of a melyrid beetle, *Carhurus elongata*, or by various wasps including the chalcid wasp *Antrocephalus stokesi*. There are also a range of infections that kill codling moth at various stages.

The following are a list of measures that will control *some* of your codling moth. Use a few of them to keep your codling moth numbers under control. All of them combined with the 'hunt them out' techniques above should eliminate all your codling moth. Note that apples crowded together are more likely to be badly infested with codling moth. Try thinning out your apples, to make it easier for predators and for your own inspection.

Caterpillar control

- Once caterpillars have finished feeding, they travel down the branches and trunk looking for a place to pupate. Trap caterpillars by scraping the loose bark from the trunk and main branches of the trees. Fix either a corrugated cardboard band or a pile of old wool to the trunk, at least 10 cm wide and soaked in liquid derris or old sump oil. Inspect every week and get rid of trapped pupae. The most important time for trapping is winter and spring, but for effective control inspect the bands all year.
- Grease-banding trunks and large branches may inhibit larvae looking for places to cocoon. Bands should be in place from the first moth sighting to mid-winter.
- Run animals under your trees. Avoid sprays that may kill other predators. A wide range of birds feed on caterpillars, as do spiders, ants, many types of wasps, hoverflies and their larvae, and the combined effect of these can be dramatic.

Moth control

- Lure pots will tell you if the moths are active. They are an ineffective method of control in themselves, as not all moths will find them. But they will give you an idea of when to spray, and how bad your codling moth infestation is.
- Spray as soon as you find your first moth and for two weeks after the last one has been dispatched.
- Fill glass jars with one part port to seven parts water, or one part molasses to ten parts water. Top up with a little oil to deter mosquitoes and stop moths from escaping. Hang them in the

trees about shoulder height in the warmest part of the orchard, where codling moth are likely to be active first. Renew the contents every week—or after every large rainstorm—and inspect for drowned corpses every morning. Other moths may be attracted to the bait.

- In large orchards you can use pheromone traps which attract and trap the males. Pheromone traps can cut down infestation to five per cent, but they are not so successful in small areas.

Spraying

The organic grower uses a derris spray as soon as the first moth sighting is made. This will kill the moths hiding in the foliage. Unfortunately it is unlikely to kill the caterpillars in the short time before they disappear into the apples.

Don't spray derris more than once a fortnight. Spray in crevices and under the leaves, as that is where the moths will be hiding, not on top of the leaves.

If the temperature is under 24°C, use a light oil spray. This will destroy eggs, but will also damage foliage in hot weather. Spray above and below the leaves every ten days.

At the same time spray Dipel directly onto the apples. This is *Bacillus thuringiensis*, a bacterial warfare on caterpillars. Continue this weekly until no more moths are trapped by your lures. It will have only a limited effect, because the caterpillars disappear into the apples so soon, but will add to the general destruction, and is less harmful than derris, which will kill other inhabitants of the orchard.

The plant-derived insecticide ryania is commonly used in the northern hemisphere to control codling moth. It is reasonably species specific, although it will kill beetles and other caterpillars, but it does kill the caterpillars after they have burrowed into the apple.

Unfortunately ryania is far less effective in hotter, harsher Australia. It is worth trying, if you can get hold of it, but don't rely on it for a total kill.

Prevention

There are two companion plants that aid codling-moth control: nasturtiums and parsnips gone to seed. Both rely on attracting predators that eat the moths and caterpillars.

I know of no trials of the nasturiums, only folklore. Flowering parsnips under the trees and through orchards have been tried in several places (including my own small plot of apples) and is extremely successful. Let the parsnips naturalise. They are hard to grow at first. Their seed lasts only a year at most, and much commercial seed is no longer viable. But I've found that once the first sets seed, and the seed blows around the orchard, parsnips spring up all over the place. A few seasons of this and they should be flowering most of the year. Slash them as you would grass occasionally, and let more flower-heads spring up.

You might also care to try non-specific insect repellents such as lavender under the trees. Some growers have reported success with these.

If you can run hens or other animals under your trees to clean up fallen apples, you will go a long way to controlling codling moth, as apples with affected centres may fall early and be eaten before the larvae can emerge. Sheep and other apple-eaters, such as wallabies, are also good under trees.

Last resort

As a last resort, dwarf apples can be grown commercially under moth-proof netting. Though this requires a lot of capital initially, it is cheaper in the long run than repeated spraying. Dwarf trees bear sooner and may be planted more closely, and yield per hectare may rise.

Ferment flies

The tiny fies that hover round your fruit bowl are probably ferment flies. They won't attack unbroken fruit on the plant. Don't worry about them.

Fruit fly

If you have warm weather and ripening fruit, be it oranges, loquats or tomatoes, you will probably get fruit fly. Unlike conventional control, where a few regular sprays will do the job, organic fruit fly control requires stringent garden hygiene as well as repellents or controlling sprays.

There are two sorts of fruit fly common in Australia: the Queensland fruit fly and the 'Mediterranean fruit fly. Both have similar lifecycles, and you are required by law to control them.

Control of fruit fly

Garden hygiene   Ensure that every bit of fallen fruit, every squashy overripe tomato, is picked up within a day, and either fed to animals, covered with water or placed in an airtight, sealed garbage bag in the sun until the fruit inside decomposes.

Sheep, chooks, wallabies and wombats are the best controllers of fruit fly in south-eastern New South Wales. We pick our fruit only when it is ripe. Fruit infected by fruit fly tends to fall from the tree before it is ripe, as the larvae burrows to the centre of the fruit, damaging the core and causing it to fall. Once the fruit is on the ground, the animals compete for it.

However, most fruit fly breed in fallen fruit, once it has squashed on the ground. Clean this up (and make sure you don't have rotting fruit in your compost heap) and you'll have also cleared up most of your fruit fly problem. In areas with long, cold winters, prevention may be all that is required. Fruit fly die off in cold winters, and garden and orcharge hygiene may prevent them from building up to problem proportions until your summer crops are harvested.

Avoid early-ripening crops such as loquats in bad fruit fly areas These may attract the fly to your later crops. Avoid late-maturing varieties that fruit when large numbers of fruit fly are likely to be around. Be careful, too, of late summer fruits, such as quinces, figs and medlars. They can host fruit fly and provide a bridge for the fruit fly to breed in, ready to infect winter crops such as citrus. A fruit-fly-free gap of a couple of months may be enough to save later crops from infection.

Separate your ripening fruit We 'time' our orchards here, so that our early fruit is separated from the later-ripening fruit. But if the ripe fruit was allowed to stay on the ground, breeding fruit fly, we would still have a problem. Fruit fly can fly five kilometres, and our methods couldn't cope with a large influx of them.

Never plant a tree that will fruit just when a neighbouring one is finishing. Let them fruit all together or allow a month between crops.

No matter how good your prevention, you may inherit someone else's fruit fly problem: a neighbour's, perhaps, with peaches dropping from the tree, or over-ripe tomatoes sludgy on the ground. In such cases other measures will be necessary.

Repellent

Fruit fly repellent is effective. It certainly keeps away fruit fly and possums, dogs, cats and Aunt Maud, who's come to smell the flowers. The smell is overpowering. But it works—with small outbreaks of a few pests.

Mix 1 litre of kerosene, 1 litre of creosote and a packet of mothballs. Place it in tins about 10 metres apart hung from fruit trees or in the vegetable garden, at about 4-metre intervals. If you can't get a whiff of it, you probably need more tins.

Bait

Fruit fly fly for about a week before they mate and lay eggs. If you can kill them in this time, you'll break the breeding cycle. Baits and traps are very effective, and provide the continuous control needed. Their main disadvantage is that they may attract fruit fly into your area before they normally would have come.

Dak pots are a commercially available trap. Forget about them. They are useful only to indicate if you have got fruit fly. They are no use at all as a control. Dak pots attract only male Queensland fruit fly. The Mediterranean fruit fly is the only one active in Western Australia, and it's the female that lays eggs: one lone male survivor can cover an awful lot of territory.

Anything sweet, wet, and yeasty attracts fruit fly. The easiest bait is fruit juice with a pinch of yeast—or even beer. Home-made ginger beer is best of all, but not commercial ginger beer: fruit fly are no fools. You can also try cut-up oranges, banana skin and/or kiwi fruit in water with a pinch of yeast, or bran, sugar and hot water.

Splash-on bait   This is made with 50 g sugar in 1 litre water. Add 7 ml concentrated pyrethrum or nicotine. Splash on the trees— *don't spray*—the result will be too dilute to be effective. Apply two weeks before and one week after the known fruit fly dates in your district, or until two weeks after the last fruit has been harvested. Re-apply every week at least, for pyrethrum breaks down on contact with light, and the nicotine will also be effective for only a few days. Commercial splash-on bait uses maldison. This is not organic but, as it doesn't touch the fruit, it can be used as a last resort.

Open traps   Fill cans or jars with the mixture below and scatter round the garden. If you find dead bees or wasps in them, use closed traps instead. I prefer closed traps anyway: why poison when drowning is as effective? But for those who feel happiest when they've applied something poisonous, mix a teaspoon of molasses (not sugar or honey—molasses is less attractive to bees) with a pinch of ground pyrethrum in 125 ml water. Or mix 10 g yeast in 5 ml water with a pinch of pyrethrum. A few drops of yellow food colour or a drop or two of oil of citronella is supposed to make the mixture more attractive to fruit fly. Scatter round the garden and check regularly, replacing the bait every couple of days.

Closed traps   These are the most effective of all. Take an empty, plastic soft-drink bottle. Cut off the top at the shoulders, turn the top over so that the neck is sticking into the bottle. Tape the edges firmly. Fill the bottle a third full of bait, cover the hole with mosquito netting, and suspend from trees or stakes in the garden.

Alternatively, just fill a plastic bottle half full of bait, hang it neck downwards, and punch a few very small holes in what is now the top. You need many closed traps to be effective: one or two won't lure the pests from the fruit.

Light-brown apple-moth

Although the light-brown apple-moth was mentioned as a pest as far back as the 1890s, it is only since the large-scale use of pesticides after World War II, especially the changeover from lead arsenate sprays to DDT, that it has become a major problem.

The light-brown apple-moth is a native pest, mostly of stone fruit, apples and pears, but also occasionally infesting citrus. The moth also feeds on many ornamental plants, wattles, clover and weeds, such as blackberry and docks. In commercial areas, capeweed has been shown to be an important host in winter.

It is soft, sappy growth that is vulnerable to the light-brown apple-moth, either soft growth on young trees, or the young 'spring' flush, especially where trees have been fertilised in early spring, or overwatered. The moth larvae spin webs in rolled-up leaves and feed from this shelter. Mostly they eat young leaves, and young trees in particular can be badly damaged. Sometimes blossom is attacked, or fruit scarred with long stripes. These are only shallow, but they can cause the fruit to rot after harvest, or make the fruit unsaleable.

Light-brown apple-moth is a cool weather pest, and damage is worst when cool weather extends into summer. Damage gets progressively less as the weather gets hotter and drier; and hot, dry summers stop it altogether. Most problems occur in cooler areas: Victoria, tableland NSW and Tasmania.

Like codling moth, light-brown apple-moths don't travel far. They frequently travel from tree to tree, and even the larvae may do so, but rarely travel any distance. Moths usually move from native plants or weeds to orchard trees in late spring, and back again in autumn. In many orchards early spring damage has been associated with spring die-off of weeds. The larvae have nowhere else to go.

Light-brown apple-moths are small, the females with a wing span of about 18 mm and the males a bit smaller. They are slightly tubby-looking moths, pale-brown and furry, with ornamented front wings and plain back ones. The moths start to fly at dusk. Twenty to thirty eggs are laid at a time. They are pale greenish-yellow and very hard to see. The larvae, who cause the damage, live and eat for about six weeks, although this may be less in warm conditions. They then pupate for about two weeks, and the moths then lay eggs for about two weeks, usually in several batches, though they may live longer in cool weather.

Light-brown apple-moth numbers build up in autumn, when orchard spraying stops. The autumn eggs hatch, and the larvae feed on weeds or wattles or stored fruit. In spring they attach themselves to young fruit-tree leaves.

Identifying light-brown apple-moth

Look for leaves stuck together with webs, shallow scars on fruit, webbing round the top of the fruit, and small caterpillars that hang from threads when disturbed. You may also catch light-brown apple-moths in codling moth traps. See page 46.

Control

Large numbers of light-brown apple-moth are a problem of over-spraying, especially for codling moth. As a native pest, the light-brown apple-moth has a wide range of predators. If you get a build up of light-brown apple-moths, it is a good indication that there is something wrong with your regime—spray drift from outside, perhaps.

Spiders are excellent predators of light-brown apple-moth, and the visible presence of spiders is another sign of a healthy orchard. Egg pathogens and parasites also keep down numbers, and a larvae virus, as do two tachinid flies *Voriella* sp. and *Zosteromyia* sp., and wasps, especially *Apanteles* and *Xanthopimpla* sp.

Common preventative advice includes clearing weeds (especially capeweed) and native species from around the orchard, so the light-brown apple-moth doesn't overwinter. This, however, is exactly contrary to good natural pest control. The presence of the light-brown apple-moth on the weeds through winter (when they are not doing any harm to your crops) is a good recipe for attracting early predators, which will also be useful for other pests in spring. The weeds will also play their own role in attracting predators and feeding their larval stage.

However, this will work only if, firstly, there are plenty of predators, and no major spraying to kill them; and, secondly, that you make sure there are plenty of ground covers in spring, when many weeds and other annuals die off, for them to move onto. In the typical monoculture orchard, where there are only weeds (which get ploughed up in late winter or die naturally) and fruit trees, the pests must of course move onto the trees.

No control measures should be needed for light-brown apple-moth in a well-managed organic orchard. If through no fault of your own, you find that the numbers are building up in apple orchards, the control measures given for codling moth should help to take care of the light-brown apple-moth.

In citrus and other crops, try squashing infected leaves and avoiding early spring growth flushes by mulching at the end of winter. This will slow down the warming up of the soil and reduce the amount of available early spring nitrogen. As the mulch gradually decays and the nutrients are made available, the tree will grow in a much steadier manner, without the sudden rich flush from warmth and nitrogen.

Pear and cherry slug

Pear and cherry slug bothers humans a lot more than it bothers the trees. While it can defoliate trees in bad cases, it rarely kills adult trees unless they are otherwise stressed as well, and shouldn't affect adult trees unless they are stressed by drought, waterlogging, overfeeding, etc, and won't affect the fruit.

The small, black slimy pear and cherry slug is really the larvae of a sawfly wasp. These pests 'graze' on the tops of leaves, chewing off the top tissue so the leaves turn brown and skeletonised and start to curl. Cherries are the most common tree affected, and of course pears, but plums and apples can also be attacked, and hawthorns in particular can attract pear and cherry slug and act as a reservoir of infection.

Damage by pear and cherry slug often appears far worse than it is. Both the trees it most commonly affects, cherries and pears, fruit on old wood. Neither should be pruned once established, and cherries are killed more often from too much care (feeding, watering and pruning) than from too little. In fact, pear and cherry slug can often have a beneficial effect, actually cutting back lush growth of cherry trees that have been heavily fertilised.

In addition, most cherries have fruited by the time they are infested with the pest. Pear and cherry slug doesn't harm the fruit, and rarely harms an adult tree, as long as it isn't further burdened by drought, poor soil or other stress. Concentrate on good management for your cherry tree, keeping the soil moist, but not wet, keeping the area around it mown with an occasional light mulch (which is all the feeding cherries need once full grown) and try to ignore the skeletonised leaves.

Pear and cherry slug is worst in cool, moist areas, where it can be a pest from spring to late autumn. Even in hot areas, however, unseasonally cool or moist conditions may mean an infestation.

The parents of pear and cherry slug are glossy black sawfly wasps, about 8 mm long. The female slits the leaf tissue and deposits the small, flat eggs into the leaf. These hatch in about two weeks: minute white larvae, narrower towards the tail. These grow to be green to black, about 12 mm long, extremely shiny and slimy and bulbously sluglike at one end.

There are two generations of pear and cherry slug each year. Some areas will be affected by both, some by only one. The first larvae appear on fruit trees in early summer. These become adults in December and January. The second generation is usually more of a pest than the first, more numerous and widespread, flying considerable distances or carried by the wind. Not all the second generation grow to adulthood at once. Some will stay on the tree and then overwinter underground.

Natural predators

Attempts to introduce pear and cherry slug predators in 1928 and 1931 failed. However, I have noticed a wide range of natural predators.

The most effective predators appear to be wasps, one of the pollistes paper wasps. These actually gather up the slugs and take them off, paralysed, to feed their larvae. The wasp colonies here can get quite massive, up to several metres wide in rock underhangs (also the kitchen window), and when the pests are on the cherry trees most of their insect harvest appears to be pear and cherry slug, abandoning the spiders that were their favourites before. These wasps, however, would probably be unsuitable as commercial predators. They are very vulnerable to insecticides.

Yellow robins also eat pear and cherry slug, with blue wrens, shrike thrushes (who are mostly fruit-eaters here) and the leuwen honey-eater also feeding on them. Given the amount of pear and cherry slug these birds eat, it is reasonable to suppose that other birds in other areas will also turn to pear and cherry slug if they are readily available. Many birds appear to notice insects only when they are numerous, and then their diet may dramatically change towards them.

Like many predators, the wasps and birds appear to make inroads into the pear and cherry slug population only after they have become a serious pest, i.e. after the tree is already badly marked by the slugs. If you are worried about the cosmetic appearance of your tree, natural predators won't be of much use to you.

In early February I searched all our cherry and pear trees in vain for a pear or cherry slug to photograph. I couldn't find any, and had to content myself with a photograph of pear and cherry slug damage, of which there was ample evidence.

The natural control was sufficient to stop the pear and cherry slugs overwintering here. This year we were back to the normal pear and cherry slug pattern: no pests from the first generation, and damage appearing only in February as adults from the second generation flew or were blown down from the hawthorn hedges on the tableland above.

Control

The best control for pear and cherry slug is to plant your cherry trees away from the house, where you won't notice the curling brown leaves. Once you have picked the cherries, don't visit the trees until they are dormant and need spraying.

Unless the trees are dying or severely knocked back, don't bother with spraying at all. Most sprays will simply kill the wasps that will control the problem for you. Even organic sprays that break down quickly will interfere with your natural pest control. For natural pest control to be effective you need pests to feed the predators. Predator numbers won't build up without a build up in food supply. If you start using any sort of control, you may have to continue using it.

There are times, however, when more control is necessary. Young trees in particular can be vulnerable to any setbacks, and pear and cherry slug will certainly set back young trees. In times of drought or other stress, too, trees may not be able to tolerate the stress of partial defoliation.

There are several organic sprays you can use for pear and cherry slug control. All break down quickly and harmlessly. In addition, there is a range of mechanical tricks you can try, at least with small trees. The slimy nature of pear and cherry slug makes them very vulnerable to dehydration. Lime (but not too often, or the soil beneath the trees will become unacceptably alkaline), dry wood ash (ditto), or flour browned in the oven will all kill the slugs. What they won't do is prevent reinfection, or kill the eggs still waiting to hatch on the trees. Unfortunately, too, unless your trees are very small, dusting their tops can be almost impossible.

Other controls include glue spray, derris spray, hellebore spray, garlic spray, pyrethrum or feverfew spray, rhubarb spray, oil spray, quassia spray.

Oil spray

Oil sprays work by covering insects or their eggs with a light film of suffocating oil, especially in winter, when the outsides are more porous. Oil sprays cause leaf damage over about 24°C. While pear and cherry slug will probably infect your trees when the weather is hotter than 24°C, oil sprays may still be used on hawthorn hedges, where some damage to the foliage doesn't matter. Pear and cherry slug often spreads from hawthorn hedges to orchards.

Scale

You'll probably notice the damage scale do before you notice the scale themselves: withering young shoots, brown leaves, splitting bark and what's known as 'general loss of vigour' in your bush or tree. Generally, this means they look like they have a hangover or galloping consumption. This can be caused by scale, as they suck up the contents of plant cells, and in some cases inject toxins into the plant. Like all sap-suckers, scale excrete large quantities of honeydew, which encourages sooty mould.

There are over 500 species of scale in Australia, both native and introduced (the cochineal scale, for example, was introduced to help control prickly pear), and most can be identified only with a magnifying glass. Some, such as the armoured scale, have hard, protective covers, while adult soft varieties such as waxy scale usually have tough or waxy tops.

To the average grower they are all simply 'scale', tiny scale-like hordes on leaves, twigs and trunks. It is often hard to appreciate that things so small can cause so much damage.

Main types of scale

Red scale are a major citrus pest, particularly in dusty orchards where the leaves have a light film on them. Sometimes, leaving a grass cover under trees instead of ploughing can drastically reduce red scale. Red scale (you can identify them by their colour) inject a toxic saliva as they feed, and trees can suffer a lot of damage quickly with yellow falling leaves, splitting bark, dying twigs and branches.

San José scale are hard to see, because they are much the same colour as the twigs they feed on. But if you run your finger over them they'll feel rough. Use a magnifying glass and you'll feel the scale. San José scale affect stone fruit, apples, pears, tree lucerne, willows and other ornamentals and often plague organic (and other) orchardists in spring.

White louse scale are another major citrus pest, mostly on trunks of mature trees. Twigs and even branches die back, but plagues are usually obvious, white lice crouched on the trunk, for example.

Wax scale infest evergreen fruit trees such as citrus, mango and guava, as well as persimmons, pears, quinces and a range of ornamentals. They produce honeydew, and in humid conditions the black sooty smudges of sooty mould are almost inevitable.

Black scale appear on evergreen trees and bushes, as well as melons and pumpkin foliage. Oleander, hibiscus, gardenias, perennial daisies and passionfruit can be affected. Sooty mould is the worst affect of black scale.

Natural pest control

Natural pest control of scale involves encouraging the predators while discouraging a population build up of scale. Methods include the following:

(a) Reduce spraying that may kill off predators. There are often large increases in scale populations after the use of organophosphate poisons, and also after the use of Bordeaux spray. This copper-based spray is commonly used by organic growers in winter for problems such as curly leaf, shot hole, bacterial blights and brown rot. Any copper-based spray will also kill off ladybirds, which is one reason for the early spring build up of scale in many orchards.

If scale is a problem in your area, don't use Bordeaux in late winter. Try several earlier sprays instead. If you must spray in late winter, spray only every second tree. Wait ten days, then spray the rest. In this way some predators will survive to breed and spread.

(b) Encourage native and other diverse species. These will harbour predators and colonies of scale to feed them. Like all natural pest control, you need to encourage *some* pests to feed you predators to avoid a population explosion.

(c) Avoid windbreaks of osage orange, japonica, hawthorn and tree lucerne near orchards. These are major hosts of San José scale.

(d) Try to keep ants at bay if you have black or brown scale. Place grease-bands round the trunks of trees and shrubs so they can't climb up. Grow rue, tansy or wormwood at the base of trees. Ants also deter wasps from gathering scale.

(e) Keep plants growing strongly. Insect pests seem to be attracted to unthrifty trees, and a healthy tree can withstand scale damage until predators start to control them. At the same time, avoid high-nitrogen fertilisers and over-watering; anything that encourages soft, sappy growth will also encourage scale (and other pests).

(f) Cherish your predators. Natural predators of scale include introduced and native wasps, ladybirds and their larvae, lacewing larvae and a small blue metallic-looking fly, *Cryptochaelum icerae* (it doesn't have a common name). Bees sometimes remove a scale waxy coating in spring. Birds are particularly good scale-gatherers, especially eastern spinebills, silvereyes, yellow-tailed thornbills and many others. (See pp. 28-33.)

The best way to deal with scale on pot plants or if you can reach them is to knock them off with a wire brush, or squash them between your fingers. They aren't as tough as they look.

Scale can be gathered to make bug juice. It is hard to collect scale without collecting leaves too. Don't bother too much about this, but remember to allow for the mass of the leaf when adding water. To make scale bug juice, gather your scale, blend them in a sieve or blender, add an equal amount of tepid milk (most recipes use water, but I find milk more effective), leave 24 hours and spray. This recipe supposes that the scale will find their squashed comrades unattractive; or that one of the squashed may be host to a disease or parasite and the bug juice will help spread it.

Try spreading diluted clay. Use just enough clay so the water looks dirty. Use only pure clay, not dirt, or you may end up with more scale than you started with, especially red scale. The clay helps suffocate the scale.

White oil or homemade oil sprays are a traditional remedy against scale. *Use these as a last resort*, because they also kill some of the scale predators. As with Bordeaux, if you must spray, do every second tree, wait ten days, and spray again. Oil sprays should be used in late winter or early spring. Don't use them when the temperature is over 24°C or you'll burn the foliage. If you are in any doubt, spray in the evening or in dull weather. Never use oil spray on blossom (it will damage it) or on fruit (it will blemish it). Oil sprays work by covering insects with a film of oil that suffocates them. The same principle works with soapy water and clay spray, but oil spray is more persistent, thorough and effective.

The best scale control is to have healthy trees, lots of birds and other species, and not to panic until the predators take over. If scale persist, try soapy water, mustard spray, onion spray, glue spray, garlic spray, quassia spray or pyrethrum spray.

Thrips (Thrips imaginis)

These are a native species. They have become an orchard pest in the last seventy years, feeding on blossoms on fruit trees so that less fruit sets. They are one of 400 thrip species described so far in Australia (some preying on other pests). They are small insects, less than 2mm long, with long, soft bodies. Some are parthenogenetic (don't need males to breed).

Thrips are often blamed for damage caused by frost or drought or bad cultivation practice. A few thrips seen feeding on the flowers are an easy scapegoat, although it is true that even four or five thrips per blossom will reduce the fruit set. They are sap-suckers, feeding on blossom, and can be found on nearly every flower from ornamentals through to weeds and trees, though they can sometimes also be seen on young leaves. Nymph and adult thrips pierce plant surface cells and suck, so that blossoms turn brown as they feed on them. Thrips can enter flowers before or after they open. Thrips are actually present in some quantities throughout the year, but they only become a pest during flowering.

Spring thrip 'plagues' usually follow damp autumns and mild winters, so that hibernating thrips can overwinter, with a dry sunny spring with plenty of weed flowers, such as Paterson's curse and capeweed. A rainy spring means fewer thrips: they are killed on the blossom and fail to emerge from wet soil. A cold snap in spring may mean that your thrips suddenly disappear.

Adult thrips are just over a millimetre long, and just visible with the naked eye, thin and light coloured with long wings. They lay eggs in blossoms, the yellow nymphs are even smaller. They feed on the petals and stamens and pistils of the flowers, then pupate about 5 mm underground. A generation of thrips may take two weeks to over a month, depending on the temperature. Thrips can fly long distances, but if alternative food is available they usually won't travel far, even in an orchard area.

Natural predators
Many birds, wasps and other predators eat thrips, but the weather is the most noticeable thrip control. Even a short burst of thrips in the blossom may cause a lot of damage before predators can control them.

Control
The best control for thrips is a large number of ground covers flowering at the time your fruit trees blossom. If you design your garden or orchard in the ways suggested earlier in this book there will be plenty of alternative blossom for thrips when annuals die off in spring.

Spraying thrips should be avoided, as it will also affect bees and subsequent pollination. Try heavy overhead watering if thrips are noticed in the blossom. It may also be worth while controlling flowering weeds, such as capeweed, just before your trees start to bloom. Don't destroy them, just whippersnip or slash their tops off. Don't control flowered weeds while the trees are actually blooming, as you might cause your thrip population to shift from the weeds to your fruit trees.

If necessary, the following sprays will kill thrips. Use them in the order given, going on to more powerful ones only if the others fail to give control: clay spray, glue spray, oil spray, onion garlic spray, garlic spray, oil sprays in cool weather (not on blossom), quassia spray, soap spray, derris spray, pyrethrum. An oil and pyrethrum spray may be used in winter if thrips have been persistently bad the year before, but like all preventatives this should definitely be a last resort. Warning: don't use oil sprays and Bordeaux mixture within a week of each other.

Wait for rain or hot dry weather to reduce numbers. Wasps, lacewings and ladybirds will keep the numbers in control after that.

Note that some thrips are predacious, and eat large quantities of mites and other small insects. Others live only on decaying matter and fungi.

Two-spotted or red spider mite

This mite became a pest after DDT and other pesticides were more widely used. Pesticides killed the mites' natural predators, such as lacewings, ladybirds, predacious thrips and mites. Until then two-spotted mites rarely invaded trees, and then usually only temporarily, when the weeds beneath crops died off. Once spraying stops in an area, and natural predation returns to normal, two-spotted mite numbers appear to decline, so in a couple of years they are no longer a pest.

Two-spotted mites are sap-suckers, piercing leaf cells. Leaves look dusty, and finally turn reddish-brown, sometimes rolling up from the edges. In bad cases, the tree may be partially defoliated, fruit may be small and badly coloured. Mite infestation is particularly important where trees bear on new growth. Loss of autumn leaves can mean less root growth and less new wood next year, and so less fruit. In general, too, infested trees are less vigorous and more prone to other pests and pathogens.

Two-spotted mites are worst in hot, dry summers, when grass and other plants are already stressed. Heavy rain (or even frequent heavy overhead watering) quickly reduces mite numbers. Apple, pear and peach trees seem the worst affected. Generally, citrus and apricots and plums are invaded only when nearby trees carry large mite populations.

Adult two-spotted mites are just visible to the naked eye, about .05 mm and greenish-yellow, with a spot on either side of the body. Eggs are laid on leaves. Two-spotted mites can lay up to seventy eggs in their lifetime, and a generation takes only one or two weeks, depending on the weather, so mite populations can increase quickly.

The mites appear in autumn, although in warmer areas they may never appear at all, staying green and feeding throughout the year. They are overwintering mites. They don't feed in winter, but simply congregate under the bark, preferably in the crotch of the tree or even where a bird has pecked fruit. They become active again in spring and move down to weeds, change to green, and start to feed on leaves and flowers.

Mites feed on a range of weeds and grasses, and move up to the trees only when these die off, starting at the bottom of the trees and working up.

Natural predators

These are the most important controllers of two-spotted mite. In fact the presence of two-spotted mite as a pest in your orchard or garden is a sure indicator that there is something wrong. Either you don't have the diversity to support enough predators, or your trees are being affected by spraying, either yours or the drift from someone else's.

A predatory mite, *Typhlodromus occidentalis*, resistant to many common insecticides, was introduced from North America in commercial orchards. It has been very effective. Native predators include small black ladybirds and their larvae (*Stethorus* sp.), a range of birds, hoverflies, predacious thrips and a range of small wasps.

Control

Control of two-spotted mite should always be as a specific and short term as possible so as to encourage predators.

Preventative measures include scrubbing old bark off trees in winter, or even covering with the old-fashioned remedy of a paste of clay and cow manure. This stops mites overwintering. Sticky bands at the base of trees in early spring will also stop the mites travelling up. Make sure, too, that ground covers are maintained throughout the year, that you don't have a sudden drop in weed numbers in late winter. This is important, to control other pests as well as mites. Supplement the weed species with your own ground crops. See 'A Healthy Garden' (pp. 9-11).

Once the mites have infested your trees, try heavy overhead watering. If this is insufficient, try a range of sprays. Try these in order, resorting to the most long lived and powerful only if the earlier ones fail to give sufficient control: clay spray, glue spray, buttermilk spray, onion spray, onion garlic spray, coriander spray, turnip spray, parsnip spray, pyrethrum, powdered sulphur. Oil sprays are effective in cool weather, but shouldn't be used in hot weather or within a week of using Bordeaux mixture. Check that the mites are still there before acting: the damage they do to the foliage won't disappear even when the pest is controlled.

You should control weeds by mulch on them or by slashing, or better still make sure you have alternative ground covers. Large orchards may purchase predator mites: *Typhlodromus occidentalis* (check with your local Department of Agriculture). They are useful only for large areas, as they need a large supply of mites to survive.

Woolly aphids

Woolly aphids usually affect only apple trees badly enough for control to be necessary, although they will also infest ornamental shrubs (especially if they are in poor condition, in shady spots or too heavily pruned), crab apples, hawthorns and occasionally pears. Woolly aphids can cause a great deal of damage on apple trees, reducing the quality and quantity of the fruit and reducing the general vigour of the tree. Like all sap-suckers, woolly aphids also excrete honeydew, which can encourage sooty mould.

Woolly aphids settle mostly in colonies, often on damaged parts of the tree. They feed by piercing the bark and sucking sap. As they feed on the shoots, small lumps appear, which later crack, and buds are destroyed. Trees infested with woolly aphids have much less new growth.

Woolly aphids are worst in cool, moist seasons, although you can find an infestation at any time. They are worst on trees with shady interiors or shaded by windbreaks or other trees. They also seem to be attracted to trees injured by animals or by unhealed severe pruning.

The woolly aphids on your apple tree are probably all wingless females. Although they appear white, they are really brownish purple and covered by white threads secreted from their bodies or a greyish powder. The wingless females produce about 100 flat brown larvae. Winged females appear in autumn.

Aphids overwinter as immature aphids on roots and near the ground on tree trunks, although a few may also survive farther up. In spite of the autumn winged form, woolly aphids are mostly spread by windborn larvae or carried by people on clothes, boxes, etc.

Natural predators

In unsprayed orchards, natural predators are usually enough to keep woolly aphids under control, as long as trees aren't injured by over-pruning or animal damage. Ladybirds, lacewing larvae and syrphid fly larvae all eat woolly aphids, as does the introduced tiny wasp *Aphelinus mali*. Unfortunately this wasp is often affected by orchard spraying, although colonies on unsprayed hawthorn hedges appear to keep the wasp surviving.

Woolly aphids that have been parasitised by the wasp lose their woolly covering and turn black. These are most commonly seen from mid-summer to autumn. These black woolly aphids should be collected in autumn, or before the birds get them, or before the first frost has driven them to shelter, say in a netbag in a shed. They can then be tied to trees that are likely to become aphid infested in spring, to speed up the natural spread of the wasp. This is especially necessary if you spray your trees in autumn. Although the wasps appear to survive oil sprays and some at least survive Bordeaux sprays, some are killed by them.

Control

Other control methods include using resistant stocks, such as northern spray for the root-infesting form of woolly aphids. If necessary, try a dilute clay spray, anise or coriander spray, or derris, rhubarb leaf, garlic and elder or pyrethrum spray in soapy water.

Other fruit problems

Apple dimpling bug   The symptoms are dimples in apples. This is purely cosmetic damage. Don't confuse it with a deeper, corky dimples of bitter pit. Rely on bird and wasp predators where possible to control it. Try bug juice if you are really worried, or quassia spray, but dimpling does not harm the fruit.

Apple scab   The fruit becomes deformed with dark-brown corky patches. To control it, spray with Bordeaux when dormant or with full-strength urine. Spray again at bud swell if the problem is severe. One-in-ten urine can be sprayed in the early morning when the tree is in leaf to stop the problem spreading. Add extra potash to the soil. Try spraying chive spray, horsetail, casuarina or seaweed sprays throughout the year as a preventative.

Apricot freckle   This starts as scabby patches on the fruit, which may join together and crack the fruit open. For control, see brown rot.

Bacterial blight of walnuts   The symptoms are black spots on leaves, black withered nuts inside. Spray with Bordeaux in winter or at leaf fall and bud swell for bad cases, or spray throughout winter with urine every two weeks. Try regular seaweed, horsetail or casuarina sprays every month as prevention throughout the year.

Bacterial canker   The symptoms are dark splitting bark, and dead wood below. It will possibly exude gum. For prevention, spray with Bordeaux when the tree is dormant, or with lilac, horseradish or elder sprays at leaf fall and bud swell. Spray preferably just before or after pruning. Canker usually starts from pruning wounds, and can lead to the death of a limb. Contrary to popular advice, summer pruning (unless you need to cut off a major limb) is better than winter pruning, as wounds recover more quickly in the summer. Cut off infected wood and paint with Bordeaux paste.

Bacterial gummosis   The symptoms are pale splotches on the leaves and oozing gum from trunk and branches. To avoid this condition, prune as little as possible, and dip secateurs in vinegar in between trees. Spray with Bordeaux in winter or with lilac, horseradish or elder or double-strength garlic at petal fall, mid-winter and bud swell. Avoid spreading the infection.

Bacterial spot   The symptoms are light-green spots on leaves; small scabby cracked spots on fruit. As prevention use Bordeaux at bud swell. Use regular elder, nettle, horsetail, seaweed, lilac, chamomile or casuarina sprays on foliage to stop the problem spreading.

Banana weevil borer   Make sure newly planted suckers are free from grubs. Clear debris away from the base.

Bitter pit of apples   The symptoms are sunken circular areas in the skin of the apple, and soft, granular flesh underneath, which breaks down quickly in storage. Bitter pit occurs when apples do not take up enough calcium as they mature. It can be precipitated by heavy pruning, too much nitrogen or a very dry season. It is a long-term problem. Add dolomite to the soil as a long-term solution: it may take up to two seasons to work. Add wood ash and seaweed mulch if handy. Try a foliar spray from compost or comfrey every second morning for two weeks.

Botritis   The symptoms are soft, watery, pale, rotten strawberries. This fungus occurs in moist, sheltered areas. Prune off some of the foliage, especially if this might have been stimulated by too much nitrogen-rich fertiliser. Spray with half-strength Bordeaux late at night when it's cool. Use chamomile tea, horseradish spray or lilac spray any time.

Brown rot   Fruit is covered with a brown rot, sometimes covered with grey spores. Brown rot may also kill blossom, especially in wet years or hot humid springs, and lead to poor fruit set or dieback of twigs.

To prevent brown rot, spray the trees with Bordeaux, horseradish or lilac spray in winter. In bad cases, spray both at leaf fall and bud swell. Prune off any dead wood when the tree is dormant and in particular any twigs that may have died from brown rot, and make sure any dried fruit 'mummies' are removed too.

Regular seaweed, horsetail or casuarina sprays can be given every month throughout the year to prevent brown rot or to stop it spreading. In bad years you may need to thin out the fruit so none is touching. If brown rot starts, pick out affected fruit at once so the spores don't spread. Spray with chamomile tea or chive tea every two days, or garlic spray once a week, until all fruit is picked. Regular spraying with seaweed spray may make your fruit more resistant to brown rot.

Fruit may be dipped in hot water after picking to stop post-harvest rot. You will need to experiment with the temperature to avoid the fruit shrivelling.

Brown or septoria spot on citrus   The symptoms are clusters of small brown spots joining together, often after autumn rain. As a preventative, spray with Bordeaux or one-in-ten urine or horseradish spray in autumn or at petal fall. Try seaweed foliar spray every three weeks as a preventative or a general plant tonic spray (see recipes, p. 136). Try chamomile sprays after rain.

Cane spot   The symptoms are purple spots on berry canes. Spray with Bordeaux mid-winter or half-strength Bordeaux at bud swell to avoid cane spot.

Canker   The symptoms are dark blackish bark, split stems and dead wood. Canker results from spores entering a pruning wound or other injury. A winter Bordeaux spray will kill canker spores on the tree. Spray before pruning. If canker is a problem in your area, paint large wounds with Bordeaux paste. Cut out affected wood and paint with Bordeaux paste.

Caterpillars   Encourage predators such as spiders, birds, wasps, etc. Use Dipel or white pepper spray or dust leaves with ground rock phosphate. Spray with glue spray, soap, quassia, ryania, pyrethrum or garlic spray only if they really seem to be damaging the plant. Try dusting the leaves with flour. This bloats caterpillars and acts as a stomach poison.

Citrus melanose   Fruit is scabby and leaves develop brown blotches within yellow patches. Limes are more subject to melanose than other citrus. To prevent this condition, spray with Bordeaux at petal fall. Cut out all dead twigs, remove all weeds near the trees and mulch heavily, renewing the mulch at least every six months.

Citrus root-rots (*Phytophthora citriodora* and others)   The symptoms are that foliage starts to die, often on one side only; the tree dies from the top down, foliage yellows and dulls. This is worst in wet weather, and trees may improve as the soil dries out. The first symptoms may also be noticed in dry weather, when injured roots no longer bring up enough nutrients. Improve drainage and channel water away. Keep up high humus levels in the soil by thick mulch.

Compost may inhibit root-rots. Use trifoliata rootstock, which is resistant to phytophthera root-rot. In bad cases, cut the tree back to healthy wood and use a foliar spray to feed the tree until the root system can re-establish. Be warned: you may control the rot with compost, but in wet years or if the compost regime is not continued the tree may start to die back again. Once symptoms appear you must always be vigilant.

To control the problem you may need to cut the tree back and feed it with foliar spray. Apply compost liberally. Improve drainage. You may choose to dig out the tree and expose the hole to sunlight to stop the problem spreading.

Citrus scab   These symptoms are raised scabby spots on fruit. Spray with half-strength Bordeaux in autumn or at petal fall or one-in-ten urine spray any time to stop the condition spreading.

Collar rot   The symptoms are that the tree dies back, yellowed foliage, lifted bark at base of tree. Don't mulch up to the very base of the tree. Avoid injury to the trees while mowing or digging. Apply compost.

Cut back all dead wood and bark. Paint with Bordeaux paste. Spray ground with double-strength garlic or lilac spray. If necessary, spray with seaweed spray every week to strengthen the tree while new bark forms at the base. Make sure new trees are planted with the bud union at least 10 cm above ground level. Keep grass and mulch at least 10 cm back from the trunk to avoid moisture collecting there and possible injury to the tree from close mowing.

Curly leaf The plants affected are peaches and almonds. The symptoms are pink or green blisters on leaves.

This can be prevented, but not cured. Spray with Bordeaux, double-strength garlic spray or lilac spray at leaf fall and bud swell, or simply once with Bordeaux in the middle for mild cases. Once the blisters have formed on the leaves, they will stay there. They are unsightly, but not harmful. Unfortunately, the same fungus can also cause premature fruit drop. If the curly leaf is affecting new leaves, or young shoots are dying back, pick off all affected leaves and spray with chamomile tea, casuarina tea or horsetail tea once a week for three weeks. Seaweed, casuarina or horsetail spray can be used every month throughout the year to prevent curly leaf.

Curly leaf is worst in wet years. It is possible that planting garlic under the trees will inhibit curly leaf, although this isn't likely unless the tops are regularly cut.

Fruit tree weevil The symptoms are wilted branches, sudden or gradual die back of the tree. The larvae of this weevil chew large furrows out of fruit tree roots; the tree may be weakened or show signs of dieback. The adults eat leaves and stems and lay eggs in folded leaves.

Remove any branches that overhang near the soil. The larvae pupates in the soil, and the adult must climb up the branches of the tree to breed. Place grease-bands or glue-bands on all branches and trunks to break the breeding cycle. Arrange a fly wire or hessian 'skirt' round the base of the tree to capture the adults as they emerge from the soil. As long as you can prevent them climbing the tree, the cycle will be broken. Make sure heavily laden branches don't touch the ground or weeds around the tree provide alternative access.

Fusarium wilt of passionfruit The symptoms are that the vine suddenly wilts, and stem of the plant rots at ground level.

Prevent fusarium wilt by planting only passionfruit grafted onto resistant stock or by covering the ground with clear plastic for three weeks before you plant the vine. Add wood ash or compost to give the soil added potash for greater resistance to fusarium wilt, as will a companion crop of broad beans.

Paint the base of the stem with Bordeaux paste. Spray soil around the plant with double-strength garlic spray. Keep the plant growing strongly with compost and mulch.

Gall wasps The symptoms are round galls on branches produced by the tunnelling larvae of the gall wasp. To prevent gall wasps, encourage bird, ant and spider predators. Cut out galls and burn them.

Grey mould and leaf spot on berries Spray with Bordeaux when the bushes are dormant, and keep bushes well mulched. Bushes can be sprayed with chamomile tea or casuarina spray at any time, every few days if symptoms appear. Cut off all affected fruit and foliage.

Hard raspberries   These may have been sucked by harlequin beetles. Thin out vines and clear away debris that may be sheltering the beetles. A band of turnips can act as a decoy crop for harlequin beetles. They love the turnips and may not go past them. As a last resort, try pyrethrum spray.

Hazelnut blight   The symptoms are blotches on leaves. This leaf disease can be controlled with a Bordeaux spray in winter. Mulch well and don't intercrop. Hedges plants result in increased retention of leaf litter—a natural mulch.

Lemon scab   The symptoms are misshapen or 'horned' fruit with scabby tops. These are caused by a fungus attacking the fruit soon after it is set. Spray at petal fall with Bordeaux; experiment with one-in-ten urine spray also at petal fall.

Lichen   Lichen is a symbiotic association of fungi and algae. Lichens can be green to grey; scaly or bushy; soft, hard or stringy. If they bother you (they won't bother the plant much unless they nearly cover it), scrub them off, or spray Bordeaux in winter, making sure in the case of evergreens that you avoid foliage and flowers. Paint it on thickly if possible.

The Bordeaux will kill the lichen, which will gradually flake off. For a faster result take up the scrubbing brush again. It is possible that lichen actually improves plant growth.

Mealy-bugs   The symptoms are tiny wax-covered ovals, and wilting leaves and shoots. Mealy-bug secretions may encourage sooty mould. Control the ants that bring them with grease-bands at the base of the tree. Encourage ladybirds, lacewing larvae, chalcid parasitic wasps.

Prune off affected foliage if possible. Use oil sprays if the temperature is under 24°C, or soapy water in the cool of the evening. In hot weather try glue spray in the evening, though not on blossom. Common insecticides don't kill mealy-bugs during most of the year because of their protective coating. Don't try. In early summer, however, you might have success with onion, pyrethrum, quassia or garlic sprays.

Mouldy berries   This is common after rain. Pick ripe berries as soon as the rain stops. Remove mouldy ones to stop them infecting others. Spray the rest with strong chamomile tea.

Oriental fruit moth   The symptoms are that shoots shrivel; and larvae may tunnel into the fruit. Stone fruit, pears and quinces are also affected.

See codling moth for preventative techniques (p. 43). Rely on wasp, spider and other predators where possible. Cut off affected twigs, use cardboard or hessian bands around the tree from December onwards. Inspect for sheltering insects every two days. Remove and destroy infected fruit at least twice a week. Scrape off loose bark and keep rubbish away from the tree. Try a clay and manure coat for the tree in winter.

Passionvine hopper   This is a small, brown moth with partially transparent wings. It lays eggs in the vine shoots where suffocating sprays can't get to them. Leaves wilt, fruit shrivels and honeydew with possible sooty mould grows on the excretions of the hopper.
Cut off affected shoots. Spray with pyrethrum, derris or garlic spray.

Pawpaw dieback   The tree dies back from the top. This dieback is common and the exact cause not known. Cut the plant at a healthy spot, spray with double-strength garlic spray, top with a tin can so the rain can't penetrate, and hope.

Peach rust   The symptoms are rusty, dark-orange spots on leaves. To prevent rust, spray with Bordeaux when dormant. Cut off affected leaves. Spray with strong chamomile tea.

Phylloxera   Phylloxera affects grapevines. it is an aphid that forms galls on the root of grapevines, greatly reducing vigour and eventually killing them. Its spread is limited in Australia so far. Be careful about taking cuttings if the area may be affected. Contact the Department of Agriculture if you want vines from other areas to find out what areas are affected. Grown vines on resistant stock. (See also aphids, p. 38.)

Phytophthora cinnamomi in macadamias   Phytophthora in macadamias produces symptoms similar to collar rot. Mulch, cut out affected areas and paint with Bordeaux to prevent other infections. Grow only in well-drained soils and keep up levels of organic matter in the soil. Use compost as much as possible to suppress the pathogen.

Powdery mildew   Leaves and buds are covered with a greyish powder. It is particularly prevalent in Jonathan apples.
Prune out affected, withered or dead shoots in winter and spray with Bordeaux, baking soda spray or Condy's crystals when dormant. Urine spray may also be effective. Add extra potash to the soil. Pick out infected leaves. Spray the rest with strong chamomoile tea, then use regular seaweed, casuarina or horsetail spray until leaf fall.

Prune rust   The symptoms are powdery brown spots under the leaves. Spray with Bordeaux at bud swell. Pick off affected leaves. Spray under the leaves as well as on top with double-strength garlic spray or soluble aspirin.

Quince fleck   This is a fungus disease, with black spots on leaves and cracked fruit. Train trees to a single, open-branched stem to allow light to penetrate. Don't plant quinces in a humid, sheltered spot, near a fish pond, for example, or an often-watered vegetable garden. Spray with Bordeaux at bud burst, and make sure all infected leaves are burnt or composted. Avoid overhead and irregular watering.
When the symptoms appear on foliage, spray with chamomile tea or elder, garlic or lilac spray to stop infection spreading.

Raspberry leaf rust   These are rusty patches on canes. Spray with Bordeaux when dormant. Pick out infected leaves and spray with soluble aspirin.

Root-rots   Root-rots are usually indicated by wilting foliage, especially in wet weather, or by gradual or sudden dying back of the tree. Root-rots can affect most plants. *Phytophthora cinnamomi* is cinnamon fungus, which affects a wide range of plants, from trees to carnations. Large roots are dark and brittle, small roots are absent. With *Armillaria* root-rots, a white fungal sheath grows over the roots, and small yellow toadstools may appear above ground. Trees with root-rots are usually shaky when you push them. The best prevention for *Phytophthora* is not to bring it in on muddy boots, infected water, bulldozers and nursery stock. Ask your nursery what they do about it. If they answer 'Eh?', buy somewhere else.

For all root-rot prevention, keep up levels of organic matter in the soil. Mulch is especially useful. Avoid digging in undecomposed organic matter such as manure or green manure. Compost is excellent and inhibits root-rots. Add dolomite to raise the pH, and use blood and bone or hen manure as high phosphorus fertilisers to keep plants growing strongly.

Make sure drainage is good. Use no-dig methods round trees to avoid injuring roots. Mulch and mow instead of digging. If you can't improve drainage, grow trees in a sloping mound on top of the ground instead of digging them in.

Avoid harsh artificial and high-nitrogen fertilisers. Encourage the microflora in your soil, imitating rainforest conditions as far as possible: such as high levels of undisturbed organic matter, moist soil with no sudden, sodden bursts from overhead irrigation.

Once your trees have been infected with root-rots, try cutting them back as an emergency measure, so the damaged root has less to support. Give the trees a foliar spray once a week (seaweed spray is excellent), or cover some good compost with water and spray it at weak-tea colour.

With luck, this will keep the tree growing while you work on the major problems: improving drainage and soil pH, mulching with good compost or lucerne hay or wilted comfrey until the natural micro-organisms in the soil can get the rots under control and the roots re-establish themselves.

If trees must be dug out, remove *all* the roots and burn them. You'll need to dig well beyond the drip line to make sure you have all of them. Leave the hole open to the air for six months at least. A large fire on the site before replanting will ensure all infected debris is removed.

If only one tree is infected, it may be worth while digging it out at once before infection spreads, especially if it is uphill, where water will carry infection down.

Armillaria root-rot can be prevented by making sure all old tree roots (orchard trees, wattles, etc.) are removed before replanting. If the trees do become infected, expose the roots for about 60 cm around the trunk to sunlight. Cut away dead roots. Fill the hole with fresh soil when infection seems to be clear. Don't replace it with mulch or compost, or water may pool in the hole. Use a slightly richer feeding regime than usual or foliar feeding till the tree picks up vigour.

Shot hole   Leaves develop small brown ringed holes; fruit is covered with small red blotches. See brown rot (p. 65) for prevention and control.

Silver leaf   Plums and apricots are very susceptible to the wood-rotting fungus silver leaf. This releases a toxin that travels through the tree. The leaves turn silvery, and branch after branch may die.

Silver leaf is best prevented by not pruning in wet weather and covering all cuts with Bordeaux paste, or spraying with Bordeaux just before or after pruning.

There is no conventional cure for silver leaf. An old remedy is to slit the back of the tree with a pruning knife down through the cambium layer and into the wood. This should be done in winter for up to four years. I don't know how effective it is.

Split fruit   Avoid overhead watering and fluctuations in moisture levels. Make sure soil is well drained.

Stink, horned and other bugs   These sap-suckers are oval or shield shaped. Stink bugs smell. They also emit an acrid fluid that can sting. Shoots and even branches may wilt, and the tree becomes generally unthrifty.

Control weeds around the trees by mulching, weeding or slashing. Clear away old pots, wood heaps, fences that may harbour colonies near your trees. Reflective foil mulches around the trees should deter the adults. Predators of bugs are a range of parasitic fungi, wasps, birds, ladybirds, lacewings and hoverfly larvae.

Try bug juice to control them. This is particularly successful with bugs, as you can easily get enough to juice. Pick off the bugs by hand. *Wear gloves* for stink bugs. Place cardboard shelters or bits of old hose around the infected plants. The bugs may shelter there during the day. Check them daily. Hose trees with as strong a spray as possible, especially under the leaves, or shake the trees. Pick up and squash fallen bugs.

As a last resort, try garlic, quassia, wormwood and rhubarb leaf or pyrethrum sprays. These will last only a few days. If the trees are being recolonised with bugs from elsewhere, they will appear not to work. The other measures above must be used in conjunction with the spray to prevent reinfection. See also Bugs (p. 78).

Strawberry leaf spot (several diseases)   Several leaf-spotting diseases attack strawberries, and all need the same preventative measures and treatment. Mulch strawberries thickly. Avoid overhead watering: use drippers or a hose poked under the mulch.

In bad cases, thin out the leaves to improve air and light penetration. A half-strength Bordeaux mixture can be used when cropping has finished for the year. Otherwise, spray with elder, lilac or chamomile sprays or double-strength garlic.

Sun blotch virus   This virus affects avocados. The symptoms are yellow or red streaks on fruit, bark and leaves.

There is no cure. Buy from reliable nurseries only. Dig out affected plants at once and burn.

Verticulum fungus; black heart of apricot   The symptoms are dying branches and leaves turning yellow early.

Don't grow apricots near tomatoes, capsicum or potatoes, as spores can be transferred. If in doubt about the soil where you are planting apricots, cover it for three weeks with clear plastic before planting.

Vine and elephant weevil   These tunnel into berry canes. To control cut out affected canes and burn them.

Wood-burrowing moths: borers   The symptoms are holes in the trunk, usually seen after the larvae has left. Sawdust deposits indicate it may still be in there. Bordeaux spray is an effective repellent. Use if necessary on sickly, borer-prone trees. Prise the borers out of their holes with a piece of wire, or inject some insecticide (derris, pyrethrum) into the hole. Fill holes with grafting wax or putty.

Wood rots   This can affect most trees. Thin frilly fungi or dark dead wood are the main symptoms. Most wood-rotting fungi attack only dead wood, injured branches or unhealthy trees. Waterlogged or starved trees are particularly susceptible. Take care when pruning, make sure drainage is good, and keep trees growing steadily.

Cut out all the affected wood down to healthy tissue. Keep the plant growing strongly so that healthy wood closes over the wound as soon as possible.

Woody passionfruit virus   Don't confuse this with cold damage, where fruit is empty. Woody passionfruit have a thickened rind, where cold-damaged fruit doesn't. Fruit is dry, leaves may be a mottled yellow.

There is no cure for this virus, but strongly growing vines are less susceptible. Fertilise with compost and mulch, and make sure they have plenty of room to spread and adequate moisture. Dig out infected vines and don't replant passionfruit there. Be careful that your secateurs aren't infected. Dip in vinegar or boiling water.

CHAPTER 3

The Pest-free Vegetable Garden

Dig as little as possible. Digging disturbs soil microflora and ground-dwelling predators.

The no-dig garden

Lay newspaper on the ground, cover with a handspan of compost, and plant in that. Better still, lay some lucerne hay below the compost. I have made a no-dig garden by slashing high weeds, raking them off, laying down newspaper, then replacing the weeds with a thin covering of compost or old sawdust on top. This had to be watered with liquid manure for a month, but worked well.

A no-dig garden has fewer weeds. Weeds colonise disturbed soil: the more you disturb it, the more weeds appear. If you can't pull a weed out of your garden when it is damp without digging, you need more organic matter in your soil. Mulch: don't dig.

Planting rules

Let plants go to seed. This will mean that you always have flowering plants to attract predators, your own cheap seed, and hardy plants suited to your area. Surround your garden with predator-attracting shrubs. Grow some flowers in the vegetable garden. These will attract predators and help crop rotation, as they are likely to be different species from your vegetables. They are also beautiful.

Rely on compost and mulch for fertility. Healthy soil really does mean fewer pest problems. Practise garden hygiene. Gather anything diseased or fruit-fly infected and seal in a plastic bag till decomposed.

Companion plants for the vegetable garden

Vegetable gardens contain mostly annuals, so their position is constantly shifting. Try shifting pots of companion plants—especially scent maskers such as aromatic herbs—near vulnerable plants. You might also consider a hedge of pest-repelling plants such as lavender or rosemary around the edges of the garden, and paths of plants that increase plant vigour, such as chamomile and yarrow.

Garlic planted near celery and silver beet is reputed to help leaf disease if regularly cut (I have never found this particularly effective).

Nasturtium flowers repel aphids from crops *above* them. They are useful only for tall crops, such as broad beans, in the garden. Nasturtiums also repel whitefly and beanfly, but only if the beans are taller than the nasturtiums. Try climbing beans.

Spent Chinese cabbage can be used as a trap crop for aphids. Try growing them around a susceptible crop such as early broad beans. Sage and wormwood are reputed to repel carrot fly. Rue may deter harlequin beetles from raspberries. Carrot fly will be repelled by onions, leeks, rosemary, wormwood and sage. Catnip may repel ants that may bring in aphids.

Celery, hyssop or scented geraniums will repel white cabbage butterfly, as will companion crops of white and red clover. These also add nitrogen to the soil. Cabbage grown with red or white clover will also have fewer aphids, as well as fewer cabbage with butterfly caterpillars, due to interference in colonisation and more predators, especially ground beetles. Try growing a patch of red clover in spring, mowing it short, and planting your brassica seedlings in a narrow, deep-dug trench. Keep the clover short as the brassicas grow, then when they are a finger high, let the clover flower. If it has been regularly cut it will flower while it is quite short and not compete with the brassicas—but it will repel cabbage white butterflies. Cabbage white butterflies are also repelled by celery, hemp and sage.

Crotaria helps control eelworms; mustard a range of nematodes. Yarrow is said to give plants resistance to insect attack. Try yarrow paths. Corn planted with sweet potatoes may increase the number of parasitic wasps preying on leaf beetles. Corn planted with beans tends to increase the range of predators for the pests of both plants. Cotton or sesame grown with corn reduces the incidence of heliothis caterpillars (corn ear worm) by increasing the number of predators.

Peanuts grown with corn tend to increase the number of spiders, leading to fewer corns borers and other pests. Corn grown with

peanuts is less likely to be infested with bud worm caterpillars
due to more spiders.

The shapes of pumpkins and corn grown together seem mutually
to confuse pests and interfere with their flight paths. The scents
of tomatoes and cabbages grown together appear to mask each
other, and especially confuse the diamond back moth.

Carrot fly is inhibited by onions, leeks, alliums, strong herbs such
as rosemary, wormwood, sage, salsify. Don't plant carrots in a straight
line. Marigolds repel white fly, as do nasturtiums and other strongly
scented plants, but I find the shape and size of marigolds and
beans go well together.

An abundance of various *weeds* appears to reduce the number
of aphids and cabbage white butterfly caterpillars on brussel sprouts,
beanfly on mung beans, stinkbugs on soybeans. Weed cover needs
to be manipulated so it doesn't interfere with cropping while still
providing diversity.

Major vegetable pests

Aphids

See in 'The Pest-free Orchard' for a more detailed coverage (pp.
38-43).

Aphids on vegetable crops can often be prevented by timing the
crop. This year, for example, I had one self-sown broad bean plant
that came up six weeks before the ones I had planted. It was covered
with aphids until early winter. The aphids didn't harm it, and it
bore at the same time as the rest, which weren't touched by aphids
at all, even though they were only a few feet away from the first
plant.

Cabbages and cauliflowers are less likely to be attacked by aphids
if they, too, are planted later in the season. Early beans may be
aphid-infected, but faster growing. Ones planted later will be less
susceptible. If your areas are infested with aphids, don't plant the
next lot until early autumn. Don't forget that most aphid predators
are active later than the aphids. Warmer weather means more
predators.

Aphids are sap-suckers, settling on growing surfaces and under
vegetable leaves. Beans particularly can be affected, as well as broad
beans, peas, vines and grass. Try deterrents such as reflective aluminium foil mulches. Late-sown broad beans, for example, are less
susceptible than early ones. French beans sown after November

are less likely to be severely infested by aphids.

The bean root aphid is a pest on coastal areas, attacking roots and underground stems. Plants may be stunted if they are growing poorly anyway. Usually a vigorously growing plant can cope with bean root aphids.

Control

Try reflective aluminium foil mulches or strong jets of water, especially under the leaves, or aphid traps. Try a dilute clay spray, seaweed or nettle spray. Use marigolds as a companion crop. Spray with nettle or seaweed spray. Elder, onion, glue, quassia, lantana, rhubarb, marigold, nettles, derris, lantana, rhubarb and elder sprays also kill aphids. Turnip or parsnip spray kills pea aphids. A washing soda and soap spray can be used in cool weather.

Beanfly

The best beanfly control is a compost-rich soil. Beans in soil lacking in potash are particularly susceptible to beanfly. Beanfly are small, metallic black flies about 2 mm long. They are often seen sitting on bean leaves or beans to lay their eggs, puncturing the tissue, usually at the leaf base. The larvae then tunnel down the leaf into the stem. You can see the tunnels as a fine tracing on the leaves, or stripes going down the stem just under the surface.

Eggs hatch after about three days in mid-summer and the new adults will be laying their own eggs three weeks later, although this may take months in cold weather.

Beanfly are worst in hot humid weather, and where there has been a succession of bean crops, so that numbers build up. French beans are most susceptible, climbing beans less so, and broad beans are hardly ever attacked.

Beanfly larvae move quickly, and can move from the top of the plant to the bottom in a week. Plants turn yellow, wilt and often die, although they may survive with deep cracks in the stem. Older plants are more resilient than young ones, and in large plants the larvae may only move down around the branches, which snap off, leaving the main plant untouched. Beans from infected plants tend to be rubbery and tough.

Beanfly are vigorous flyers, and are also carried by the wind. Even if there are no other bean crops near you, autumn beans are likely to be infested if you have been growing a succession.

Natural predators

Wasps and small birds, such as robins, can nearly clean up an infected patch of beans. Beetles, spiders, damsel bugs, hoverflies, lacewings, ladybirds and their larvae, mantids and stilt flies may also reduce the numbers.

Control

- Try adding potash or compost to the soil. Often beanfly can be controlled just by improving the soil.
- Hill plants around the base to encourage new roots. This will let the beans recover after an attack.
- Avoid successions of beans in bad beanfly areas. Try an early and a very late crop only, when low soil temperatures slow down the beanfly breeding rate.
- Plant climbing beans instead of french beans. These may be attacked, but the death rate is much lower.

Try traps of sticky boards, preferably yellow, covered in glue or motor oil. The flies will be attracted and trapped. Or spray just after the plants emerge, then at weekly intervals. Spray in the early morning when the leaves are flat, as they will curl up in the heat of the day and the spray won't stick as well. Try spraying with dilute clay spray first of all, then wormwood spray. If these fail, use garlic spray. Dust with derris every three days.

Budworms (Heliothis sp.)

Budworms are called tomato grubs when they appear on tomatoes, and are one of the worst tomato pests for commercial growers. Home gardeners are probably most familiar with the corn ear worm, *Heliothis armiger*, but budworms will also attack cotton and lucerne crops as well as flowers such as calendula, hollyhocks and snapdragons. They enter pods of beans or peas and eat the seeds.

Budworms are particularly hard to control organically: once they get into the pods, predators can't get at them. Neither can most organic controls. Budworms are the larvae of small, fat moths. Like most moths they start to fly at dusk, feeding on the nectar of flowers and weeds and laying eggs. The eggs are white and tiny and usually laid in young growth on the tops of the plants. The moths live about two weeks and lay up to 1000 eggs. The eggs hatch after about a week, and the larvae feed on young foliage or flowers, moving to buds or fruit as they get older. During this time they may change colour according to their host, from pale green to cream to a darker green or yellow, or even dark red or brown, with darker stripes and usually a white or paler stripe along their length. The larger the larvae the larger the holes. The larvae pupate after two to six weeks, burrowing into the soil and emerging from two weeks to five months later—longer if the weather is cold or the soil is dry. This means that in good conditions a generation of budworms may be produced in a month.

Budworms are worst in early summer or late spring and autumn. They are strong fliers, and can travel long distances to a new crop, though usually they don't fly more than 50 metres at a time.

Budworms attack tomatoes from flowering to maturity, chewing the buds and entering the fruit, usually near the stem end. The bigger the grub the bigger the hole. The fruit rots from inside.

Natural predators

Birds, wasps, spiders, diseases and egg parasites help control the early budworms stages. But as they get bigger and older they are safe within whatever they are feeding on.

Repellent

Mineral oil dabbed on corn 'silk' or on tomato branches near the fruit will repel budworms. Try dabbing mineral oil on the corn casing once a week, or spraying (the casing only) with oil spray. This will turn the casing brown and unattractive, but the moths won't lay on it and the caterpillars will avoid it.

Larvae and moth control

You need to act while the larvae are still small, and still eating leaves, not when they are big and feeding on fruit and seeds. Dipel may be used, as can any of the irritants, such as clay spray, pepper spray. Derris spray or dust will also kill the caterpillars, at least before they have burrowed into seeds or fruit.

Budworm moths are strongly attracted to light. Use a port wine trap (see Codling Moth, p. 43) to see if they are active, then try a light trap at night.

Bugs

The green vegetable bug is an introduced pest. Luckily several strains of wasp have also been introduced to control it. Bugs are sap-suckers, using their sharp beaks on stalks, stems and pods.

Green vegetable bugs, like other bugs, are shield shaped. The adults are bright green, though overwintering adults turn brown to reddish-black. These become active in early spring, feed on new growth, and several generations may be bred during the summer.

Bugs usually mature in about five weeks. Peak bug numbers are usually in autumn, when you may see large clusters on plants.

Rutherglen bugs are small, grey-brown native bugs. They mostly breed on winter weeds and migrate to gardens when the seeds die off in spring. Harlequin beetles are also natives, breeding up in weeds and often congregating in large swarms on plants, fence posts, wood piles, etc. Harlequin beetles are longer than most bugs, about 12 mm, reddish-orange with black markings on top and paler below. Stink bugs can also attack vegetables. These are mostly green with brown wings. Be careful handling them: they not only stink, they can also burn your hands.

Predators

Several wasps, including the introduced *Trissolcus basalis*, a tiny, shiny black wasp about 1 mm long, lays eggs in the bug's eggs. Birds will also eat bugs (I have seen kookaburras, starlings and magpies eat them), but this does not seem to control the numbers enough to save susceptible plants in late autumn and early spring. Mantids, dragonflies and robber or assassin flies also kill bugs.

Control

Conventional advice is to control weeds around crops. I have found that as long as the weed cover is diverse, they don't all die off at once, so the bugs don't migrate into our garden. However, if we slash the weeds around the garden, the bugs move in. Try to have a barrier of annual flowers blooming in early spring, when many annual weeds die off.

I have found controlling slow 'compost heaps' (by which I mean piles of garden waste rather than true compost) more effective. Bugs seem to shelter in these piles in great numbers. Also, make sure you don't keep your wood pile near the garden. Check wooden sheds and fences too for sheltering bugs in autumn.

Try spraying plants with a strong soapy mixture in winter, especially under the leaves. This is a deterrent as well as an irritant to young bugs. A strong hosing at any time (again under the leaves as well as on top) may dislodge many bugs. Tread on them. As a last resort, try diatomaceous earth spray, pyrethrum or feverfew, ryania, derris, quassia, bug juice. As a very last resort use nicotine.

Cabbage moth

While the cabbage moth is quite different from the cabbage white butterfly (it is greyish-brown and hairy with yellow diamond-shaped markings when the wings are folded) the caterpillars of both are easily confused. Both are green, and both devastate cabbages, cauliflowers and similar crops. Cabbage moth caterpillars, however, are a clearer green than cabbage white caterpillars and lack the velvety appearance and yellow strip.

In terms of garden control, however, the difference is slight. Cabbage moths also lay their eggs on the underside of leaves. The cabbage moth caterpillar tends to eat towards the heart of the vegetable, and may cause even more damage than the cabbage white.

Predators

Like cabbage whites, the cabbage moth caterpillars have predators in the form of a range of imported wasps: different ones from the cabbage white's. Native wasps don't appear to be so particular, and I have noticed two species here that will carry off either. The same range of birds also appears to attack both.

For control, see cabbage white butterfly (below).

Cabbage white butterfly

The cabbage white butterfly is a European import. It first appeared in Australia in 1939, and soon became a major pest of all cabbage crops, as well as wallflowers, stocks, occasionally mignonette and nasturtiums and a range of weeds, such as mustard. In warm areas cabbage white butterfly larvae will feed throughout winter. In colder areas they do most damage in autumn and spring.

It is the larvae of the cabbage white butterflies that eat the leaves. The butterflies themselves feed on nectar, usually from flowers, although I have seen them on gum trees as well. The butterflies are a creamish yellow with black wingtips, and a black spot on the hindwing, about 5 cm across. The female has two black forewing spots as well, while the male has only one.

Cabbage white eggs are a pale yellow, and laid on the underside of leaves, usually near the edge. The young caterpillars hatch there and start feeding under the leaves, transferring up top as they get older. The young caterpillars are pale green with fine velvet hair and faint yellow stripes down the side. They usually feed for two or three weeks before pupating, and there may be several generations a year.

Cabbage white cocoons are light greyish-yellow to green and about 18 mm long. In cold areas, the cabbage whites overwinter in their cocoons, either attached to growing crops or just near by, and it can be worth while hunting these out and destroying them, although the butterflies can fly several kilometres, and any susceptible crop is likely to be attacked.

Predators

Three imported wasps attack the caterpillars. I have also noted several native wasps carrying off caterpillars and a wide variety of birds, as well as assassin bugs, mantids, centipedes, dragonflies, ichneumons, scorpion flies and spiders. Lacewings eat caterpillar eggs, and hoverflies may eat very small caterpillars just after they have hatched. There is also a natural virus that may reduce numbers.

In a diverse garden, you may find that natural predators are enough to control the caterpillars, but only after a wait of several weeks, while they notice the available food. There may be considerable damage during this time. Choose a means of control that won't deter the predators, such as squashing the caterpillars on the leaves, or using Dipel. The latter will leave edible caterpillars: but while sickening they will be easier to catch.

Control

- Place empty eggshells in the beds to deceive the butterflies as to their population density.
- Surround the beds with strongly perfumed herbs, such as lavender. See 'Natural Pest Control', p. 3.
- Interplant other crops so it is more difficult for caterpillars to migrate from plant to plant. The more companion plants the less damage.

Sprays and dusts

Make sure that you spray or dust the undersides of leaves as well as tops, as this is where the young caterpillars will be hiding.

Try flour first. This is a caterpillar stomach poison. It will take three or four days to be effective, however, and may be washed off before enough is eaten.

Try Dipel as the next resort, or clay spray, bug juice or white pepper spray. White pepper spray will slightly dehydrate the caterpillars, and most will die; the rest will be easy prey for birds, etc. You might also try dusting the leaves with powdered rock phosphate for the same effect. If these fail, try wormwood spray, garlic, quassia, or dusting or spraying with derris.

Caterpillar trap

This may be useful for large infestations where caterpillars denude one plant then move on to the next. Place a small, three-sided box at the base of plants, about 10 mm high. Place a scatter of lime or wood ash inside. The caterpillars should shelter there during the day.

Cutworms

Cutworms are actually the larvae of several different species of moths. They feed at night, and cut off young plants just above ground level. Probably the best known of the moths is the bogong moth. It is about 5 mm with three spots on the forewing. All the moths are nectar-feeders, often eating large amounts from eucalypts and other good honey-providers.

The moths lay pure white, rounded eggs, either on the surface of the soil, on leaves close to the ground, or on mulch or leaf litter. The eggs hatch in a few days if the weather is moist, or can remain dormant for several weeks until it rains. The caterpillars grow from 4 mm to 4 cm, and are smooth, dark pink to brown or green. They are all soft-bodied. If you dig them up accidentally, they curl up as though dead. They feed for about a month then pupate deeper in the soil.

Cutworm moths are strong fliers. They sometimes swarm, often for many kilometres. Bogongs were once a feasting food of Aborigines. Cutworms mostly infest two sorts of soil: soil that is heavily infested with weeds and flooded or badly drained ground. Several years ago my father complained of cutworms in his bottom garden; but the top garden, better drained, was untouched.

Cutworms will attack any seedlings, young weeds, vegetables flowers, cereals and even recently transplanted cuttings. They feed at night, sheltering in the soil during the day, girdling young stalks so that the plants fall over or die. Older plants may also be attacked, and will wilt or yellow, though they may recover, leaving scar tissue just above the ground.

Predators

Birds are the best cutworm predators: kookaburras, ibis, magpies, starlings, crows, yellow robins. Ground beetles (such as the cala-soma beetle and tiger beetle, bugs and a range of flies and wasps) also attack them, and in humid weather they are very vulnerable to disease.

Control
- Make sure soil is well drained.
- In bad cases let the land lie fallow for six weeks, really fallow, no weeds at all, so the lifecycle is broken.
- In commercial plots, try surrounding your land with a fallow strip, heavily baited with cutworm bait.
- Try trap crops for cutworm, such as lucerne, maize, turnips, chicory, mustard. Lift these crops (roots, soil and all) after four weeks and burn them, or leave the roots exposed to light on a plastic or paper sheet so the grubs can't return to the soil, turning them over once a day.
- Surround the paddock with mustard as a decoy.
- Lay down black plastic and leave it there until the grass and the cutworms are dead.
- Lay clear plastic over bare ground for three weeks. This should kill the cutworms.

These steps will have to be repeated if cutworm moths are still flying. The best solution is to improve drainage and increase the humus level of the soil.

Protecting the crop
If your crop is already infested with cutworms, try the following:
- Spray Dipel over the soil and plants at night.
- Splint each plant with two toothpicks so they can't be cut.
- Surround each plant with an tin-can barrier.
- Drizzle a thick molasses and water solution into the soil to dehydrate the cutworms. Don't use this too often, as too much sugar is bad for the soil. Don't use honey, as you may spread bee diseases.
- Dip new seedlings in Dipel before planting.
- If you see a recently cut seedling, dig it up at once. The cutworm may still be there and you can kill it.

Cutworm bait
Mix one part bran with one part of hardwood sawdust (not pine), then with two parts molasses and enough water to make it all moist. Spread this around the plants. The cutworms will rise to feed at night, be attracted to the bait and get trapped in the sticky

mess, unable to burrow back into the ground. They will die at sunrise from heat and dehydration, or be picked off by birds.

Earwig (European)

These are an introduced pest. European earwigs like cool temperatures and moisture, and will come inside for both. The adults are brown and about 12 mm long, with folded wings and forceps on the front. A revolting fluid can be ejected from the back, but won't hurt you. Females lay two batches of eggs, in spring and early summer, so there is usually only one complete generation a year. The eggs are laid in small nests in the soil and the females stand guard. The adults are mostly nocturnal, as are the six nymph stages. The adults rarely fly, and are mostly transported in soil, rubbish and pot plants.

Earwigs eat a wide range of fruit and vegetables: the plants damaged seem to vary from location to location. The only damage they do in my area is to eat rosebuds. They will also eat seedling roots, fallen fruit, flour, dead meat, live or dead insects.

Earwig damage usually has a 'nobbled' appearance: the leaves, buds and fruit edges are left ragged.

Prevention

Clean up piles of debris; keep slow compost piles and wood heaps away from lettuces or young seedlings, or any other water-soft green plant that might be vulnerable.

Control

- Try poisoned bran. Mix it with derris and enough water to bind it.
- Try grooved wood traps: two pieces of grooved wood placed over each other and emptied every day.
- Put crumpled paper in old pots and empty every day.
- If they are eating your rosebuds, try a sticky grease-band at the base of each bush to stop them climbing up.

Earwigs are often blamed for slug and snail damage. Other earwigs species are valuable predators of other pests.

Mites: two-spotted (red spider) mite; bean spider mite

Spider mites are one of the worst vegetable and ornamental pests, particularly attacking beans and cucumbers. They will also attack other crops (such as carrots), especially if they have been planted close to an infected bean crop. Foliage becomes webbed, with brown, dry patches. These grow till the whole leaf is grey. If you turn over the leaf, you will see it covered with mites and webbing. Leaves wilt from the edges inward. They then fall off, so the top of the plant is bare. In bad infestations the plant may die. Mite-covered vegetables look dull and grey, and will seem rubbery to touch.

Adult spider mites are only just visible with the naked eye, about 5 mm long, red and spider-like. They lay small, round translucent eggs under leaves, usually close to the veins. The larvae range from colourless to pale brown, moult and become pinkish nymphs, and moult again to become adult. Mites may mature from egg to adult in a week, and there are several generations a year.

Spider mites are worst in warm, dry weather: rain is often enough to control them. Mites are often carried from crop to crop on clothes and gardening tools, although they are also carried on leaf fragments in the wind.

Prevention

Mites dislike moisture. This is one of the times that overhead spraying is better than drip irrigation: water well and frequently. I also find that close planting with other tall species (which helps to increase humidity and makes it harder for the mites to transfer from plant to plant) seems to cut down the numbers of mites.

Mites also appear to attack plants that are starved of nitrogen and/or phosphorus. Better feeding means fewer mites. At the first sign of an infestation, try spraying the plants each morning or later afternoon (when it is cool) with a homemade liquid manure on the foliage and around the plant. Try hilling. Many crops like beans will develop more roots and so be healthier.

It may also be worth cutting the tops out of the plant. These will be worst infested, and while this won't control the mites completely (you are sure to miss enough for them to breed up again), it will at least give the plants breathing space so you can improve fertility.

If a crop has been badly attacked by spider mites, don't plant a succession crop immediately. Dig the old crop in when it has finished bearing (this is one case where digging in is better than leaving the spent crop as mulch on the ground) or compost it in a *hot* compost heap (not a pile of rubbish that will let the pests breed) and wait two weeks before planting again somewhere else.

Make sure, though, that there isn't another mite-infested crop (such as cucumbers) near the new planting site. And make sure this crop is well fertilised and companion planted and that mites aren't transferred on your clothes.

In bad cases, where you have had mites from year to year, I suggest planting marigolds between your beans (the middle-sized ones, not the miniature or tall ones) or borage sown at the same time as the beans, so it flowers with them, or any of the flowering 'deterrents' described in the section on companion planting in chapter 1.

Predators
Spider mites have many predators: ladybirds, both the adults and larvae, lacewing larvae, predacious thrips and other predacious mites, hoverflies, mantids, stilt flies and several wasps.

Sprays
Try buttermilk spray, oil spray in cool weather (under 24°C), clay spray, glue spray, onion garlic spray, coriander spray, pyrethrum. In very bad cases, as a last resort, dust with sulphur (cool weather only).

Mites: other
The broad mite sometimes attacks silver beet and rhubarb. Mite damage is often taken for leaf spot: the leaves become spotted and rusty looking. However, unlike leaf spot, the stalks are also damaged by the broad mite, and the whole plant looks twisted as though it has been damaged by herbicide. Inner leaves are usually worst affected.

The broad mite is usually worst in late summer and early autumn in hot humid weather. It is also a major pest of young citrus. Use the same control measures as the mites above. The rust mite also attacks rhubarb leaves. The symptoms are similar to those of the broad mite.

Onion maggot
Onion maggots burrow into the stems, then hollow them out below ground. The plants yellow and fall over. Onions and garlic are mostly affected, but beans, melons, cabbages, etc. can also be attacked. Onion maggots are the larvae of grey-brown hairy flies about

5 mm long. They can be seen flying over soil where manure or decomposing green matter has been dug in recently.

Onion maggots are a problem of badly prepared soil. Don't plant crops where there is undecomposed organic matter in the soil (green manure, animal manure, etc.). Leave them on top of the ground to decompose naturally and be pulled under by worms. Don't ever dig them in. Onion maggots mainly feed on organic matter, but will also attack stems, and may destroy several plants before they are fully grown.

Control

Avoid undecomposed organic matter in the soil, especially in spring and autumn. Avoid even mulching crops at this time. Apply mulch in mid-summer and mid-winter instead. Wood ash between the plants will deter the flies as will a barrier of aromatic herbs.

28-spotted and 26-spotted ladybird

Leaf-eating ladybirds shouldn't be confused with the predacious ladybirds. The leaf-eaters attack melons in particular, especially rock melons (cantalopes), as well as potatoes.

The ladybirds really do have the number of spots attributed to them, and this is an easy form of identification. They are about 6 mm long, yellow to orange with black spots. They can fly, but seem to prefer not to. They lay eggs under the leaves, which hatch in about a week, feed for three weeks, then pupate. The whole cycle takes about six weeks.

Adult ladybirds feed on the upper surfaces of the leaves, while the larvae feed underneath. Leaves can be eaten all the way through, so that only the veins are left, or can just become transparent and scarred. Sometimes pieces of rock melon skin are chewed. Ladybirds are most active in summer. They may be present in the cool weather, but do less damage.

Predators

A variety of birds, assassin bugs, soldier beetles, mantids.

Control

This probably won't be necessary except in rare situations. Sprinkle the leaves with diatomaceous earth; sprinkle the leaves with derris, use a derris or pyrethrum spray if the infestation is bad enough to stunt the plant, which is unlikely.

Vegetable weevil

The vegetable weevil attacks carrots, parsnips and celery, hollowing out roots. It also attacks cauliflowers and their family, lettuce, silver beet and spinach and a range of winter flowers, such as pansies and stocks. Most damage is done in early winter and later autumn. As the winter progresses the small, pale-yellow grubs get bigger and may even attack the crown or foliage of the plant. In late winter the grubs pupate in the soil. The adults hatch in spring, eating both tops and roots. They are inactive in summer, and lay their eggs in winter.

Grey-brown adult weevils are about 9 mm long. They are difficult to see, as they feed at night and drop back onto the soil if disturbed.

Prevention

Late summer or autumn sown root crops are most susceptible to the vegetable weevil. Try planting your whole year's crop in spring and early summer, and digging them as required. This way they will be tough enough to withstand the weevils in autumn.

If the weevils have been a problem, plant a crop of beans, peas or oats or wheat before your root crop. Avoid chantenay carrots. They seem very susceptible to the root weevil.

Weevils are parthenogenetic: you need only one weevil to breed more weevils. They are very tough and long lived, and can travel in old fruit boxes, on bits of wood and seedlings. It is worth taking some care to keep them out of the garden.

Weeds can be a host for the root weevil. Conventional advice is to grow carrots in land that has been kept weed free, and not to allow weeds round the borders of your growing area. On the other hand, a wide range of weeds (not just one or two sorts) will mean there is always an alternative host for your weevils. The real problem comes when you have weedy ground: plough it roughly so weed root remain, plant with carrots, then start weeding. The carrots are the only plants left for the weevils to feed on.

Once you have weevils you are unlikely to be able to wipe them out, either with conventional or organic methods. It is better to occupy them elsewhere—or to keep them out to begin with.

Control

Try the cutworm bait given on page 83. Other measures to control cutworms are also successful with the vegetable weevil.

Whitefly

Whiteflies appear to be just that: tiny white flies that seem to stick to leaves, especially of beans crops, but also of tomatoes, potatoes and vine crops, sucking the sap and causing the whole plant to wilt or even die. Whiteflies, like other sap-suckers, also produce honeydew, and plants can be further affected by sooty mould.

Whitefly are worst in warm, humid conditions, especially in green-houses or crowded gardens or where the air circulation is poor. They can fly from plant to plant, but are more often wind borne, often for large distances.

Predators

A New Zealand wasp predator, *Encarsia formosa*, was introduced here in 1943. The wasp lays its eggs under the skin of whitefly nymphs. Although this kept numbers down for many decades, whiteflies seem to be becoming more of a problem. Many small birds also control whitefly, as do several spiders, ladybirds and their larvae, hoverfly, damsel bugs, mantids and stilt flies.

Control

Whitefly seem to be more of a problem where the soil is deficient in potash. Try adding good compost or wood ash to the soil. I have found compost-fed plants resistant to whitefly. Make sure the plants aren't overfed with nitrogen, even compost can be too rich in nitrogen if you've added a lot of urine, or blood and bone, or grass clippings that have recently been fertilised. (Park grass clippings are often in this category.)

Aromatic companion plants will also help keep whitefly away. Try growing susceptible plants in a barrier of aromatic plants, prefer-ably flowering ones, such as marigolds.

As a last resort, try a wormwood spray, derris, onion garlic spray or pyrethrum.

Other vegetable problems

Bacterial soft rot   It leaves carrots and other root crops a soft smelly mess. It is usually a post-harvest problem, with damaged carrots stored in a plastic or badly ventilated areas. If it occurs in the ground, the carrots have probably been damaged by weeding or digging. Mulch instead of weeding, or water first and pull instead of digging. Make sure soil is well drained. Where rot has been a problem, don't replant carrots for at least three years.

To prevent soft rot in storage, dry carrots in the sun after pulling. Keep in a well-ventilated spot. If they must go into bags, use netting or paper, not plastic.

Bitter cucumbers   These may be too large, or were left on the vines until their skins started to yellow. Pick them younger and sweeter. A spell of cool weather or lack of water can cause cucumbers to turn bitter.

Bitter lettuce   Lettuce that have had any check in their growth may become bitter. Keep well watered and well fed.

Blossom end rot   The symptoms are dark, rotten patches on fruit, especially tomatoes. This is due to irregular watering or lack of calcium. Mulch well to reduce water stress. Improve drainage. Fertilise with compost. A foliar spray may increase calcium. A half-strength Bordeaux spray can also be used.

Carrot fly   The larvae burrow into the roots. Carrot flies prefer straight rows. Sow carrots in blocks not rows. For bad cases, sow carrot seed with spring onion seed, and sow both together or keep a permanent band of spring onions round your bed. Onions need to be actively growing to be effective (try cutting out the tops so more shoots grow) and you need twice as many onions as carrots, or a thick band of onions around the carrots. Compost-fed carrots are less attractive to carrot flies. There are some indications that compost made with seaweed may be even more effective.

Celery leaf spot   These are dark spots on the leaves and dark, curling leaf edges. Feed celery with compost; make sure air circulation is good. A regular seaweed, nettle or casuarina spray may prevent leaf spot. Spray leaves with chamomile tea every two days or Bordeaux every two weeks. Wash well before eating.

Chocolate spot on broad beans   Add wood ash or compost or comfrey mulch to provide potash. Spray with soapy water as soon as first spots appear. Repeat every few days, especially in rainy weather.

Clubroot   Roots are large and knobby. The plants may wilt (especially in hot or dry weather), die or just fail to thrive. Protect your crop from nematodes with a companion crop of marigolds or, better still, mustard. Mustard grows quickly. Plant it at the same time. Keep up levels of organic matter, especially in sandy areas where clubroot is worst. Try barriers of old tin cans with tops and bottoms cut out as 'root guards'. Add a sprinkle of lime or dolomite to the soil to reduce acidity. Practise stringent crop rotation for at least four years before any of the cabbage family, swedes or turnips are grown in that spot.

Cracked carrots, tomatoes, etc.   Vegetables crack with too much rain or uneven watering. Plant them in a well-drained spot, mulch so they don't dry out. Alternating very wet and very dry soil is a sure recipe for cracking.

Silvereyes may peck your fruit, but only if it has been opened by larger birds. They prefer grass seeds and small sap-sucking pests. Attract them with an unmown lawn and fresh water.

A wallaby cleans up fallen oranges in the orchard: animals beneath the trees will help keep down fruit fly and other pests.

The remains of a bird-eaten pest.

A blue-tongue lizard cleans up snails.

A green tree frog, a sign of a healthy garden.

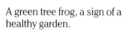

Don't destroy spiders' webs: spiders are excellent predators of pests – from codling moths to fruit fly.

Fungus spot These brown spots on leaves affect a range of vegetables. Use regular seaweed, horsetail, casuarina or nettle tea as a preventative. Fertilise with compost and improve air circulation. Avoid overhead watering. Spray with Bordeaux in cool weather; horseradish tea, one-in-ten *fresh* urine (no more than a few hours old).

Leafminer These are seen as white, skeletonised lines through the leaves. Try bug juice. Dust leaves with ground rock phosphate, onion or garlic spray. Add compost to the soil as long-term prevention.

Mildew Powdery mildew leaves a grey film over the leaves. Downy mildew makes foliage shrivel with white clumps of fungus underneath. Mulch to keep spores from splashing up onto foliage. Try not to water foliage: aim at the roots or try drip irrigation. Spray with seaweed spray to increase resistance. Use milk, chamomile, chive and casuarina sprays every few days if symptoms appear. Dust with powdered sulphur. Use Bordeaux at half strength, or baking soda or Condy's crystals. Use at night, and make sure no blossoms are touched by the spray. Use other controls first.

Misshapen cucumbers and other vegetables This may be due to poor pollination. Grow lemon balm or borage or other flowers around your garden to attract bees.

Molybdenum deficiency This mostly affects cauliflowers, but other brassicas can also suffer. Plants are stunted, yellow, with distorted leaves, and may not produce worthwhile sprouts or centres. Most Australian soils are at least slightly molybdenum deficient. Compost made from molybdenum deficient material will also be deficient. The traditional cure is molybdate dissolved in hot water and used as a foliage spray. Make a molybdenum spray by soaking comfrey or cauliflower leaves from the greengrocer in water until it turns pale green. Spray morning and dusk for three days then weekly.

Neck rot in onions This causes the squelchy, sulphur-smelling, rotten onions sometimes found in the bottom of bags of commercial onions. Neck rot enters the onion through a wound. Make sure the tops have completely withered before you cut them off. Don't use spades or forks near onions. Mulch them instead. Bordeaux mixture, if given for mildew, tends to harden the outer layers of the onion and make them less susceptible to rotting. High-nitrogen fertilisers mean soft susceptible growth.

Pea blight (bacterial) This appears as dark-brown edges or splodges on leaves. The stem may also develop splodges. Both leaves and stem may shrivel. Don't replant peas for at least three years. Use only healthy seed. Collect all infected matter from a crop, and burn or hot compost. Don't pick or weed peas in wet weather. See solutions for powdery mildew on p. 93.

Potato blight This appears as dark, brownish spots on the leaves, which increase in size with a green-white mould. Leaves die, lesions appear on the stems. Fungus spores are washed from the leaves to the tubers, which then rot. Potato blight can be carried by wind, water or infected plants.

Spray with Bordeaux in the early stages to prevent spores washing to the ground. Spray again if symptoms continue after two weeks. If symptoms appear near harvest time, slash off the tops and burn them or compost. Then spray the stalks with Bordeaux. It is better to do this and get a slightly smaller crop than risk losing the lot.

Potato gangrene   Potatoes rot from the inside with deep, rounded depressions on the outside. The smell is horrible, like rotten fish.

Plant only disease-free seed. Try not to damage potatoes when digging up or weeding. Potato gangrene affects only injured plants at harvest. Never store potatoes that are injured in any way at all, even by a scrape on the digging fork. Any injury can let fungus spores enter. Make sure storage areas are free of dirt and debris from past crops.

Potato mosaic and leaf roll   These are virus diseases carried by aphids from infected plants. The symptoms of both include rolled-leaf edges. Plants may die early, with yellow veins in the leaves and possibly mottled spots.

These viruses can't be cured once the plant is infected. Plant disease-free tubers and hope your neighbours' aphids don't carry the disease over the fence. Don't use small tubers with long thin shoots for seed potatoes. They may be infected with leaf roll. The viruses don't remain in the soil after the tubers and aphids have gone. Crops can be planted in the same soil as long as you are sure no small potatoes remain. It is difficult to be sure.

Potato moth   This moth burrows into potatoes, and may cause them to rot. Make sure no tubers are exposed, as the female moth may lay eggs in the potatoes. Hill and mulch. Spray with Dipel or pyrethrum.

Potato scab (1)   Small brown circular or oval scabby crusts appear on the potato. Potatoes may be affected under the soil, with no sign above. Plant disease-free tubers. Make sure drainage is good. Scab is worst in wet soils below 18°C. Spores can remain active for fifteen years or more.

Potato scab (2)   This may look like the scab described above to begin with, but the scabs gradually cover the entire tuber. No symptoms may appear above ground. Plant only certified seed. Common scab is introduced on infected tubers. It can also infect beetroot and turnips: these should not be grown where you plan to put next season's spuds.

Common scab is worse in dry, warm conditions and light sandy soils. Mulch well to keep in moisture and keep up the humus levels. Avoid liming your potato bed. Once scab is present, green manure your ground before planting and add plenty of compost, which will help control it. Compost and most decomposing organic matter probably encourage soil micro-organisms antagonistic to scab. Make sure soil is kept moist round potatoes, particularly when the tubers are forming.

Potatoes: soggy   These are lacking in potash. Add wood ash to the soil, but not too much as the soil may become to alkaline. Mulch with comfrey or good compost.

Potatoes: green   These have been exposed to sunlight, and they are bitter and poisonous from an alkaloidal glucocide called solanine. Don't eat them. Newly dug potatoes are most susceptible. Don't leave them on top of the ground before bagging. Store potatoes in a dark place.

Symptoms of solanine poisoning resemble gastro-enteritis. Small quantities probably won't make you ill, but it's best to be safe. Save green potatoes for seed and don't eat bitter ones.

Potatoes: eelworm nematodes   These appear as wart-like swellings on potato skins. Eelworm eggs and their larvae can survive for two years in the soil, so plant an eelworm-resistant green manure crop such as rye, wheat or oats, or plants such as sweet corn, onions, cauliflowers and cabbage, which can tolerate them. Encourage earthworms with mulch. They eat eelworm eggs and larvae. Several species of fungi encouraged by high levels of decomposing organic matter trap eelworm in mycellium webs. In other words: mulch.

Powdery mildew   Avoid growing vine crops in hot, humid weather. Keep foliage dry by avoiding overhead watering or watering early in the morning. Mulch well to stop spores splashing up onto the plant. In cool conditions zucchini may be sprayed with Bordeaux or Condy's crystals, but this will burn leaves over 24°C, and young leaves may be burnt at any time. Spray soapy water in the cool of the evenings, avoiding flowers. Spray chamomile tea at any time, or elder spray. Pick out infected leaves and burn them, or hot compost them as soon as they appear. If you have already had problems with mildew, plant a second zucchini crop a couple of months after the first in a well-drained airy spot away from the first crop.

Rhubarb: bacterial crown rot   The crown rots and the young leaves shrivel. Dig out affected plants, and burn them or put them in hot compost. Spray the rest with Bordeaux in winter. Leave holes open to sunlight for three weeks or spray with Bordeaux. Spray plants with chamomile tea or elder spray in summer.

Rust   Velvet brown pustules appear on the foliage. Mulch and avoid overhead watering, which spreads spores. Spray with Bordeaux in cool weather (under 24°C). Dilute soluble aspirin spray may be tried. Dust foliage with powdered sulphur.

Silverbeet leaf spot   The symptoms are brown spots on leaves. Keep the plants growing strongly. Pick off affected leaves and eat them. Mulch well. Spray with chamomile tea every week if you find the problem too unslightly. If this fails, try elder spray or double-strength garlic spray or Bordeaux or baking soda spray in the cool of the evening. This may burn the leaves, but will destroy the fungus, so new leaves are unblemished. But try the other remedies first.

Tomatoes: fusarium wilt   The plant wilts, rotted at the base of the stem.

Stems may be cracked. In mild cases the plant may just grow slowly or be pale and stunted.

This is a soil-borne fungus. Try covering the soil with clear plastic sheeting for three weeks before you plant out tomatoes in order to kill off spores in the soil. Or grow a crop of thickly planted broad beans as their root secretions will inhibit the fungus. Practise crop rotation. Use resistant cultivars.

As soon as symptoms appear, try double-strength garlic spray on stems, soil and foliage. Seedlings can be dipped in garlic spray before planting out, with a little drizzle onto nearby soils. Soils high in potash are more resistant to fusarium wilt. Try adding wood ash or compost. In bad cases, dig out plants and burn them. The spores are both wind and soil borne, and will easily spread to neighbouring plants. Cover the hole with clear plastic or drench the soil in double-strength garlic spray, or both.

Seedling problems

Cutworms   Seedlings wilt or the stems are chewn off at ground level. See cutworms (p. 82).

Damping off   Seedlings suddenly wilt and die, especially in wet conditions, in humid weather, or if there is a high level of undigested organic matter in the soil. There may be a narrow wilted or brownish collar near ground level.

Don't plant seedlings directly into mulch, particularly in hot, humid areas. Part the mulch instead to leave a small space around each seedling and don't pull it back until the plant is growing strongly. Make sure all organic matter in the soil is well rotted before planting seedlings. Try leaving it on top instead of digging it in. Dip seedlings and their soil in chamomile tea before you plant them. Drizzle another half cup of chamomile tea around each plant. Repeat this every two days for a couple of weeks. After this the seedlings should be tough enough to withstand damping off.

Plants yellow and wilt   These may have been 'forced' in greenhouses or affected by air conditioning. Cover with newspaper propped up on twigs until they are hardened off. Plants may also be starved of nitrogen if planted in decomposing mulch, or if the soil isn't nitrogen rich (from other earlier mulch layers) around them. Water with liquid manure or liquid compost until the mulch has broken down further. (Liquid manure is obtained by covering compost with water; use it when it changes colour.)

Young seedlings may be pecked by birds   Cover with black cotton threaded over twigs, or cover with newspaper, as described above. Try reflective foil mulch.

Failure to thrive   Seedlings may have been put into ground that is too cold; may be starved or under- or over-watered. Pine needle mulch may inhibit seedlings; many adult plants (including brassicas such as cauliflowers) excrete root or leaf substances that inhibit seedlings. Avoid old roots or plants debris in the soil near seedlings. See also slugs and snails (p. 120).

CHAPTER 4

The Pest-free Flower Garden

The same principles apply here as in the vegetable garden: feed with decomposing mulch and compost, dig and disturb as little as possible, attract predators, maximise leaf cover, include some nitrogen-fixing species if possible.

Companion plants for the flower garden

Companion planting can be beautiful. Many of the companion plants already described can be used to increase the vigour of other plants or protect them from pests.

Perfume enhancers

Chervil, garlic, marjoram, oregano, parsley, yarrow, chamomile (supposed to increase essential perfumes oils). As far as I know the reputation of these is based only on folklore.

Flower problems

Aphids

See pp. 38 and 75.

Bacterial leaf spot

The symptoms are semi-transparent circles on leaves. To prevent this occurring make sure air is circulating round the plants. Clean up infected leaves. Apply compost.

Spray affected foliage with casuarina tea or half-strength Bordeaux.

Botritis, balling and other flower rots

Cut off affected flowers. Spray with chamomile tea or use seaweed spray for prevention.

Bud grub

The symptoms are rotten flower centres. Use Dipel, pyrethrum spray, derris spray, rhubarb leaf spray, white pepper spray.

Caterpillars

See cabbage white butterflies (p. 80). Avoid large blocks of one sort of flower.

Collar rot

This causes the plant to wilt and die. Avoid undecomposed organic matter in the soil. Make sure it is composted or not dug in. Don't mulch up to stems. Don't over-water.

If the plant is affected, spray with Bordeaux in cool weather; use double-strength garlic spray in summer. If collar rot has been a problem, cover ground with clear plastic for three weeks before planting.

Crown rot

The symptoms are that the plant wilts suddenly, and the stem rots at ground level. Apply liberal compost, avoid undecomposed organic matter near stems. Use regular seaweed sprays as prevention. Raised beds may be needed.

Cut out affected plants; leave holes open to sunlight for three weeks. Try to improve air flow by cutting out low growth. Bordeaux may be effective in cool weather, or garlic spray in summer. Try drenching the ground with strong chamomile tea at any time.

Leaf eelworm

The symptoms are shrivelled, blackened foliage. To prevent this condition, increase humus levels, add compost. If the plant is affected, saturate ground with one-in-ten molasses solution or pyrethrum spray. Use cutworm baits.

Leafminer

The symptoms are skeletonised tracery on leaves. Use soapy water spray, pyrethrum spray, rhubarb leaf spray, or bug juice using pulverised leaves as well.

Mealy-bugs

Plants wilt, growth is stunted, small downy white insects appear under leaves and on roots. Control the ants with companion plants of wormwood or tansy. Practise crop rotation. Encourage natural controls such as ladybirds, lacewing larvae, chalcid parasitic wasps.

Prune off affected foliage. Try an oil spray in cool weather or a soapy water spray at night. Common insecticides won't kill mealy-bugs because of their protective coating. Don't try.

Powdery mildew

The symptoms are powdery deposits on leaves. To prevent improve air circulation, avoid transferring spores, cover infected material on the ground with mulch so spores don't splash up, practise crop rotation.

Spray affected foliage with milk spray, chamomile tea, chive tea, elder spray, double-strength garlic spray, or casuarina or horsetail tea. In cool weather use a washing soda spray or Condy's crystals.

Rust

The symptoms are raised orange dots on leaves. To avoid: improve air circulation and mulch to stop infection splashing up. Spray with soluble aspirin spray or willow water. Try chamomile tea. Bordeaux can be used in cool weather.

Shot hole

The symptoms are brown or lacy holes in the leaves. Spray with Bordeaux in winter, improve air circulation, and mulch. Use chamomile tea, chive tea, elder or casuarina spray at any time.

Thrips

See Thrips and fruit problems (p. 59).

Shrub problems

Azalea lace bug

These are shiny, 4 mm-long, black bugs. The nymphs suck sap, causing yellow or grey mottled patches on leaves with black sticky spots from their droppings. To avoid, make sure weeds don't encroach round the bushes and encourage birds. If affected, use a derris or pyrethrum spray every ten days. Make sure you spray under the leaves as well as on top.

Camellia bud mite

The symptoms are bud drop and small mites in the flowers. Control weeds such as capeweed or clover, or make sure there are other ground covers when these start to die off. Use milk spray at any time or oil spray if the temperature is under 24°C. See also Thrips (p. 59) for further preventative ideas.

Camellia rust mite

The symptoms are discoloured leaves. Control weeds or make sure there are alternative flowering ground covers. Avoid weeds underneath your camellia bushes. Milk spray at any time. Oil spray if temperature is below 24°C.

Canker

The symptoms are dieback of branches; split bark oozing gum. Avoid pruning cuts, where spores of the fungus can enter. No control is possible when the disease has got hold. Remove the tree and plant another species. As a temporary measure, cut out dead wood and paint with Bordeaux paste and feed the tree with compost and a foliar spray of homemade liquid fertiliser. This will keep the tree growing for a while, but it won't cure it.

Collar rot

The plant pales, wilts and dies and the stem is rotted at ground level. To avoid, keep mulch away from the stem, avoid undecomposed organic matter in the soil. Don't crowd the plant with small nearby plants. Don't mow or dig too near the stem in case you damage it.

If affected, cut back plant to good wood and paint with Bordeaux paste. If the collar rot has girdled the tree, you may need to 'bridge graft'. In which case, consult an expert grafter. If the plant dies, dig it out and replace with another species after the hole has been left open to the sun for three weeks or, better still, covered with clear plastic.

Cypress bark weevil

The symptoms are that the branches die back, foliage loses colour, and larvae chew holes in bark. Keep trees healthy. Bordeaux is an effective repellent for old or sickly trees. Cut off dead branches. Keep the plant growing strongly, so it can outgrow depredations. Healthy trees seem to be less attractive to the beetles. The same symptoms may be the result of the cypress pine weevil. Control is the same.

Frangipani dieback

The symptoms are hollow stems with blackened ends. This happens when temperatures are too low. The damaged areas may be invaded by insects. These will be the effect, not the cause. Try dabbing Bordeaux paste onto cold-damaged twigs.

Hibiscus beetle

These 3 mm-long, black beetles are mostly pollen feeders, although they may chew holes in petals. There is no need to kill them.

Mealy-bugs

The symptoms are white, fluffy bulges. Encourage birds and grease-band trunks to deter ants. Dab foliage with methylated spirits. Try an oil spray if under 24°C. Wipe leaves with a soapy sponge. Don't use other insecticides, as they can't penetrate the waxy coating and are ineffective.

Oak or beech blotch miner

The symptoms are brown blisters on leaves. Use milk spray, or oil sprays in cool weather, below 24°C.

Petal blight

Buds and flowers dry out until they are brown and papery. Flowers then stick on the plant until long after unaffected flowers have fallen. Cut off affected flowers at once. Spray with chamomile, chive or lilac tea as soon as flowers start to form, every two days if you have had the problem before.

Powdery mildew

The symptoms are circular white patches on leaves. To avoid, improve air circulation, mulch, and avoid transferring spores on clothing or tools. Use milk spray, chamomile tea, chive or casuarina tea. Use regular seaweed, nettle or general tonic spray as a preventative. Baking soda and soap spray may be used in winter.

Rust

The symptoms are yellow flecks on leaves and premature leaf drop. Keep the plant growing strongly. In bad cases, remove and plant another species or try to obtain a rust-resistant variety. Regular sprayings of seaweed spray or plant tonic may help. Try aspirin spray or willow water.

Salt toxicity

The symptoms are brown leaf edges. Improve water supply if it is contaminated.

Sclerotina rot

The symptoms are stem rots at ground level. Keep mulch away from the stem. Drench area with strong chamomile tea or garlic spray.

Sooty mould

Most ornamentals can be affected by sooty mould. Affected plants are covered with black patches that look as though they have been dusted with spot. This is often stimulated by the sugary secretions of aphids, mealy-bugs or scale. If you eliminate these, the problem should clear, although it may take a few months for the sooty mould to peel off.

Sooty mould is mainly an aesthetic problem and will disturb

you more than its host, although it may affect photosynthesis and reduce the vigour of the plant if it covers a wide area for a long time. Once pests have been controlled, try hosing the plant vigorously to remove scale and help the mould flake away. Use hot water if possible. A damp sponge should be used for leaves within reach.

White and pink wax scale

White wax scale produces lumps on the stems; pink wax scale produces lumps on leaves and stems. See Scale on page 56.

White cedar moth

Trees may be defoliated by leaf-eating caterpillars. Try Dipel, quassia, garlic and pyrethrum sprays. Encourage birds, wasps and other predators. See Codling Moth (p. 43).

Whiteflies

Clouds of small white flies suck at foliage and cluster on shoots. To avoid, add dolomite, rock phosphate or wood ash to the soil. White flies do best where the soil is deficient in phosphorus or magnesium. Try growing nasturtiums under the bush. If affected, wipe leaves with a soapy sponge. Use an oil spray if temperatures are under 24°C. Try attracting white fly to yellow boards covered with glue or motor oil.

Willow gall sawfly

Pale-green or reddish lumps appear on leaves. Galls are ugly, but don't harm the tree.

Pests on native plants

Many native plants have a short lifespan. Old and sickly trees are more prone to pests and diseases than healthy trees. Old and sickly trees may need to be removed.

Acacia spotting bug

Streaky brown spots are caused by sap-sucking and injection of saliva. Leaves may die in a severe attack. The bugs are yellow-brown, about 10 mm long. Spray with pyrethrum or derris in soapy water.

Aphids

See pp. 38 and 75.

Beetles

These can also be predators of a wide range of pests. Make sure they are actually badly damaging your plant before you try to control them. They are mostly easily controlled at the larval stage. See Christmas beetles (below).

Borers

These are beetle or moth larvae. The grubs tunnel into stems or roots and may cause considerable damage, which may be noticed only when an empty hole and dying branch is left. Sickly trees are prone to borer attack, so keep them healthy. If you find a borer hole with fresh sawdust, which indicates the borer is still in there, block it off with grafting wax, or skewer the borer out with a bit of wire. Lavender bushes grown around your plants may act as a moth repellent.

Healthy trees also can engulf the borer with resin as it burrows. Keep trees growing strongly. If you know you have susceptible plants, paint the trunks and main branches with Bordeaux paste diluted with four parts of water in early spring. This deters the females from laying their eggs on the treated trees.

A simple repellent is a thin slurry of wood ash painted on the tree. In desperate cases, try the following repellent. Soften 7 kg of soap in 4 litres of water for a few days. Heat till it is too hot to touch, add 500 g of flour and 3.5 kg of naphthalene flakes. Increase heat and stir until these dissolve. Cool, stir in an airtight container. Apply warm with a paint brush. This is not organic, because of the napthalene flakes. You might care to replace it with another insect repellent, such as lavender oil, but this would be very expensive in the quantities needed.

Christmas beetles

Christmas beetles attack mostly in summer, eating young leaves first and then the older ones. They seem less attracted to strongly smelling species, such as lemon-scented gum, but will eat any eucalypt in a pinch. Attacks by christmas beetles can be identified by chewed leaves, not to mention large, glossy-winged beetles crashing into your windows at night attracted by the light. Trees may eventually be completely defoliated.

Young trees with new foliage are particularly susceptible to christmas beetles and may be killed by complete defoliation. On the other hand, some young trees develop an attractive bushy appearance after constant christmas beetle pruning, so pruning new growth will help to make your area less attractive to christmas beetles. Immature christmas beetles are large white grubs with reddish heads. They eat plant roots.

Control   Shake the tree and stamp on the beetles. Spray the leaves with garlic spray, derris or pyrethrum, or tomato spray. Don't spray the beetles: they'll be relatively unaffected with their thick carapaces. Spraying their food is much more effective.

Eucalyptus weevils

These are small weevils that chew leaves. These can be controlled by wasps and other predators, which parasitise the eggs. Avoid harmful sprays that may eliminate them.

Fern weevils

These eat out stems and pupate in them. Cut out and burn infected fronds or soak them in water for three weeks to break the lifecycle.

Fungi, mildews and sooty mould

Bordeaux can be used on most native plants, except on delicate or new foliage, or where the blossom may be spoiled. In hot weather, spray in the cool of the evening. Repeated applications will be needed in wet weather. Use chamomile tea or casuarina tea at any time.

Galls on leaves or stems

These are caused by the larvae of the gall wasp, or by a parasite after the larvae. Cut off the gall if necessary. They rarely harm the tree, but some people find them unsightly. Rosellas, black cockatoos and other birds will eat them.

Kurrajong leaf roller

This is a dull-green caterpillar that rolls and mats leaves together. The moth is yellow with black markings. Use derris or pyrethrum spray while the caterpillars are young (1 kg pyrethrum or derris powder to 1 kg soft soap and 20 litres of water). Try Dipel.

Leaf spot

This is common in some grevilleas and hakeas in humid weather. Improve air circulation if you can, although it can be difficult in jungly 'native' gardens. Spray with Bordeaux in cool weather or late in the evening, or wipe foliage with a sponge dipped in chamomile or chive tea. Or spray with casuarina tea.

Mole crickets

These are dull-brown insects with black eyes, about 6 mm long, with strong front legs. They may uproot young plants and seedlings. They usually cause minimal damage, and there is not much point in trying to get rid of them. If absolutely necessary, prepare an emulsion of equal parts soft soap and eucalyptus oil. Inject this into tunnels to bring them to the surface or spread it thickly on the ground around the plant stems to deter them.

Pittosporum leafminer

These appear as small pale slightly dimpled specks on leaves. This insect only disfigures the leaves and needs close inspection to be noticed. Damage is rarely sufficient to affect the vigour of the tree.

Psyllids

This family includes lerp building psyllid nymphs, protective coverings for the lerps to shelter under. Leaves often curl after lerp infestation, and this may help shelter the larvae. They are related to aphids and other sap-suckers. Look for rounded or flat bumps on leaves. Psyllids have a wide range of predators, including many birds. The eggs are preyed upon by the melyrid beetle, *Dicranolaius cinctus*, the nymphs by the wasp *Psyllaephagus genutus*, as well as many ants species. There is probably no need to take action against them and they shouldn't reduce the vigour of the tree.

Lerps rarely build up to 'problem' numbers. If they do, it is likely to be in long, unseasonably cool weather, when predators are less active, or if there has been widespread pesticide spraying near by. Trees may be damaged, but will recover. If you spray at this time, you will simply have to keep spraying, as you will stop the natural predators building up. The tree will recover as quickly whether you spray or not. Try feeding and watering to encourage new, soft growth, unsuitable for lerps to lay eggs on. But the trees have their own defences again psyllids. Leaves that have been heavily damaged fall; new leaves grow and these are too soft to be suitable for egg-laying. Adults fail to reproduce, and as psyllids are poor flyers they usually fail to move elsewhere, there is a decline in their population. By then weather conditions should have changed, so the predators will build up. High levels of psyllid infestation appear to be associated with low tree density. The 'manna' lerp can be soaked in water or sucked. They are incredibly sweet.

Sawflies

Sawflies aren't flies, but wasps. They were called sawflies because of their sawlike egg-laying apparatus. Sawfly damage is indicated by skeletonised leaves. There are various species of sawflies that damage eucalypts, the most common being the steel-blue sawfly, *Perga affinus*, also commonly known as spitfires. When disturbed, spitfires raise their heads and abdomens and eject a thick yellowish fluid from their mouths. This hurts. It probably evolved as a defence against parasitic insects, but means the nickname is most appropriate.

Steel-blue sawfly larvae are black, and cluster together around branches. They are about 70 mm long. Eggs are mostly laid in summer and autumn. The larvae of the callitrus sawfly, *Zenarge turneri*, are green and about 10-20 mm long. Callistemon sawfly feed voraciously, but only on callistemons. They have a swordlike protruberance on their abdomen.

The leaf blister sawflies attack several species of eucalypts. They feed between the upper and lower surface of the leaves so the leaves appear blistered. Mostly young trees are affected. Infestations usually last only a season or two then disappear for some years.

Solution   The first defence against sawfly is to wait for predators. The chief of these are birds, especially cuckoo shrikes and yellow robins. A wide range of wasp species also attack sawflies. Ants are a less effective but persistent predator. If sawflies are badly defoliating the trees, try to shake them down. Use a rake to shake the higher branches. Because of their clustering habit, sawflies are easily dislodged. You may prefer to prune off lower branches that are affected. Wear boots when you stamp on sawflies or import chooks to eat them.

Even though they are not true caterpillars (larvae of moths or butterflies) Dipel can be effective against sawfly. Dipel is a bacterial derivative that attacks caterpillars' intestines, and so is harmless to predators. Dipel must be eaten to be effective, so make sure you spray the leaf thoroughly, not just the sawflies.

Derris or pyrethrum dusts will kill sawflies, also garlic spray, elder spray, tomato spray.

Slaters

These are greyish, flat and many-legged. They shelter during the day and feed on young plant shoots at night. Try a bait of one part pyrethrum to two parts of flour. This can be either wet or dry. Place near wood heaps or rubbish piles where slaters shelter during the day.

Soldier beetles

These are attracted to the flowering natives. They look obvious, but rarely damage the plant.

Spittlebugs

You will probably notice the frothy material the nymphs produce to protect themselves. The adults are sap-suckers. These do little damage, but may be hosed from the tree.

Staghorn frond beetle

These are small, round beetles with orange larvae about a fingertip in size, which tunnel into staghorn fronds. Simply cut off the infected fronds, or squash the larvae inside, and you'll very effectively break the breeding cycle.

Stick insects

Bad infestations of stick insects may defoliate and even kill a tree, but even then the stick insects may be almost invisible, their long slender bodies and spindly legs perfectly camouflaged on the tree.

Flowers planted together with thyme and healthy celery.

Let some vegetables go to seed each year to attract predators to clean up pests, as well as provide you with next year's seed.

Wire guards can be used to protect plants from flying pests; or, as in this case, to keep the hens off a patch of garden while they clean up pests and vegetable waste elsewhere.

Cut-off plastic bottles guard these cabbage seedlings against cabbage moths and butterflies – and the plants grow faster in these miniature greenhouses.

Pesticides need not be poisonous; use chillies to repel grasshoppers, flour against caterpillars, milk or mustard for red spider mites and mildew, pepper against soft-bodied insects like pear and cherry slug or caterpillars, sugar in an eelworm or fruit fly trap, and oil sprays against a whole range of pests and their eggs.

Stick insects are all vegetarian, and at least three Australian species may cause a lot of damage.

Most stick insects reproduce normally. Some are parthenogenetic. Females drop their eggs while perched on a tree, and these can even be as thick as gentle rain in autumn. The eggs lie on the ground all winter and the nymphs emerge in spring, very like the adults, but smaller, without wings and reproductive organs. The nymphs head for the trees and start eating leaves. Many will die in a dry spring, or are eaten by spiders, birds or ants.

Grease or other banding of trees in spring will stop the nymphs climbing up the trees. As they are wingless, a thick barrier will stop them. Encourage birds.

Tea tree web moth

The larvae of these moths feed on foliage together, sheltering during the day in a mass of webs. Prune off the webs and burn; spray with pyrethrum in soapy water or garlic in soapy water.

Termites or white ants

These can eat the centre out of trees. Avoid scarring trees near the base, as this can provide an entry point. Cut out infected wood and seal with grafting wax, then burn the infected material. Cut down and burn badly infected trees to save others. Try to dig the nests out whole, or cover the area with boiling water then pyrethrum spray.

Wasp galls

These appear as lumps on leaves. Most gall-forming wasps are tiny. Their larvae feed on leaves and pupate inside the gall. Pesticides (organic or not) rarely penetrate to harm them. Prune off affected foliage, if really necessary, and burn.

Wattle leafminer

The adults are small moths. The larvae cause the damage, tunnelling into the leaves, making a fine thin line or pink blister, which eventually dies and flakes off. The larvae pupate in the blisters.

Cut off affected leaves and burn them. Spray with pyrethrum spray in soapy water, although this may have limited effect as the larvae are protected in the leaves.

Wattle mealy-bug

These oval insects are about 4 mm long, purply-black with white wax stripes. They mostly feed on soft new growth. These probably won't cause great harm. Prune off affected shoots if necessary.

Wattle tick scale

These are large scale, about 5 mm across, darkening from blue-grey to dark brown. They can be dull or shiny and are usually grouped together. They will probably be cleared by predators. Prune them off if necessary or spray with garlic spray in soapy water.

White-stemmed gum moth

These large hairy moths have wavy, grey-brown markings on the wings. The larvae are about 11 mm long, with spikey tufts of hair. They rest behind the bark during the day and feed on leaves at night. These moths should cause little damage if the tree is growing strongly. Wrap sacking round the tree for them to shelter in during the day. Remove and squash.

CHAPTER 5

Some Common Pests

Ants

Ants are valuable predators. They may also transfer sap-suckers from plant to plant (to 'milk' their sweet secretions) and their nests can kill plants above them.

Prevention

Avoid ants in your garden by increasing humus levels with plenty of mulch. Keep your garden moist (again, use mulch, with drip irrigation, if possible). Move pots regularly to stop ants from building nests in and around them. I find pouring the hot tea remnants on my pot plants—as well as adding tea leaf mulch—also gets rid of ants.

Control

- Scatter a bait of one part of borax or derris to four parts of icing sugar around their nests.
- Try a spray down into their nest of one part kerosene, one part liquid detergent, eight parts vegetable oil.
- Pour a bucket of boiling water down the nest, wait ten minutes, then spray all the ants on the surface with a bought or homemade pyrethrum based spray.
- Grease-banding around shrubs or on the base of seedlings will keep ants of them.

Birds as pests

Birds should be encouraged. Occasionally, though, you need strategies to keep them from a particular crop. Any deterrent needs to last only as long as the crop is vulnerable, in most cases no more than a few weeks.

However, some birds should not be encouraged. These include starlings, which may drive away native birds, sparrows and other introduced species. Starlings and swallows are just starting to move into our district. Put nets under the eaves to keep them out. Shoot them if necessary, not for the damage they will do to your crops, but because of the birds they will displace. Try the following means of control in the order given.

Encourage resident birds

The worst fruit losses usually come from transient birds, such as white cockatoos or silvereyes in a drought. These don't spend their entire year in your area, but will move from food source to food source in large numbers. Many birds are territorial and will keep out other birds. Learn to know the ones who live with you. They may give you some protection against strangers.

For example, a friend has a currawong that feeds on her strawberries. The currawong and its friends don't start feeding until 11 a.m. She picks the strawberries at 10 a.m. and they get the squashy or earwigs-hollowed ones. The currawongs are fiercely protective of their strawberry bed, and scare off any smaller bird that approaches.

Predator birds

Eagles, hawks and kookaburras scare off smaller birds. Try feeding the large ones near your trees to deter the smaller ones. Try bread fried in margarine or dripping, bacon rinds, bits of cheese.

Provide water

Up to 40 per cent of bird damage may be halted if you provide water, preferably fresh and out of the reach of cats and dogs. Many birds that are otherwise seed and insect eaters will attack fruit if they don't have clean, safe water.

Provide alternative food

Most birds prefer slightly acid food, and often will eat native species in preference to cultivated species. However, some fruits (such as kiwi fruit, which stay acid a long time) are irresistible, and can be used as a 'barrier' for other crops. (We use old apples in a basket to keep the birds from the kiwi fruit. It works excellently.) A bird barrier crop need not be pruned or fertilised or watered.

Don't be afraid that planting more food species will attract many more birds. Birds need territories, nesting places, etc., as well as food.

Prune less or differently

Most fruit trees are pruned for picking convenience, and so fruit ripens all at the one time. This is wonderful for birds. Unless you are a commercial grower who needs to minimise picking time, don't prune the centres of your trees (V-shaped trees break down sooner anyway). Let the leaves hide most of the fruit, let them ripen over a month or so, and you will find your bird damage is much less.

Most birds don't like going into dense bushes or vines to eat, although they will happily forage under them, or nest in them. Design your garden for dense canopy areas, prune less and stake less.

Grow dwarf species

These can be hidden under nets or behind other trees. I find that birds such as rosellas and parrots avoid dwarf trees, perhaps because they are low to the ground and they feel vulnerable to predators such as dogs, cats and foxes. Dwarf trees also provide less shelter from hawks and other overhead threats.

Deterrents

There are probably as many bird deterrents as there are gardeners. Imitation snakes, old computer tape, dangling tin cans, slices of onion, silver-wine-cask bladders pumped up and dangled from the branches (very effective), strips of aluminium foil, all work to some extent. Their effectiveness diminishes with time, as birds get used to them. Hang up your tin cans, etc., as long as you need to protect your blossom or fruit, never for more than three weeks at a time (if necessary change to another deterrent).

Nets

These are not always feasible on big trees, and birds sometimes get caught in them. Try netting individual branches of big trees with old netting orange bags (and let the birds eat the unnetted fruit) or push over old nylon stockings. Our neighbours have a wide net of old stockings that they throw over ripening trees— the net doesn't protect the fruit, but it does provide a deterrent.

Tree banding grease

This can be used on any branch where a bird may conveniently perch. It will limit depredations and possibly scare the birds from the trees. Warm the grease and apply liberally with an old brush or stick.

Noise

Many commercial orchards rely on loud irregular noise from battery or gas or petrol driven bird-scarers. These are expensive, and birds get used to them. They are not suitable for suburban gardens.

In built-up areas a loud audio tape or radio may be effective for short, irregular periods. Make sure radios are turned to a 'voice' channel, preferably a sports commentary of a grand final.

Hummers

Long humming lines are now commercially available to deter birds. They can be effective. Old computer tapes have been suggested as alternatives. I tried this unsuccessfully with white cockatoos. They are said to be effective with starlings.

Scarecrows

These can work, or just become a convenient perching place. The shorter the time they are in place and the more they move with the wind the more effective they are.

Hawk kites

These are widely advertised. They are portable, easily installed. They are very successful for a few weeks, and if moved at least every three days. Birds soon get used to them, however. Small birds (including chooks) are frightened by them. Hawk kites may keep other, useful birds out of your garden. Use them for a short time only.

Ultrasonic noise

These can keep birds away—and everything else. I have heard of several cases where they have not been successful. They may be effective in commercial orchards over a two-week ripening period. It is claimed that humans can't detect them. Many can.

Foul tastes

Try spraying with a strong solution of garlic (warning: this is also a pesticide and should not be used liberally) or bitter aloe, the stuff you buy from chemists to stick on kids' fingernails to stop the kids biting them.

Commercial bird repellent, methiocarb, is poisonous to birds, humans, slugs, snails and more. Avoid it.

Quassia spray is reputed to repel birds. It is an effective insecticide and will kill aphids, caterpillars and hoverfly larvae. Use with discretion. Don't use within seven days of harvest, because the fruit will still be bitter. Cover 1 cup of quassia chips with 20 cups of hot water. Use when cool.

Flying foxes or fruit bats

The only sure way to keep off fruit bats is to buy specially designed nets to keep them out (ordinary netting doesn't work). Fruit bats usually prefer native fruit to your crops. However, growing one sort of native fruit may not be enough, and may simply attract them to your garden. They'll eat the native fruit (and fruit bats may fly long distances to feed) and then move into your fruit trees. You need to grow a wide variety of native fruits when your trees are ripening, as an insurance policy, as well as using deterrents.

• Paper bags impregnated with a strong-smelling oil, such as eucalyptus, lavender or urine over the fruit.
• Mothballs hung through the branches.
• Loud noises, especially if they are of a high frequency, until they get used to them.
• Leave the radio on a 'talking' channel, although they will soon get used to this as well.
• A fishing line can be strung between branches to confuse them.

Grasshoppers and locusts

There is no real difference between a grasshopper and a locust except that migrating swarms are usually called 'locusts'. Given good conditions, plague locusts can breed incredibly fast, with up to four generations a year and dormant eggs adding to the problem. A plague can develop in four months.

The Australian plague locust usually lives in the dry outback. It needs relatively bare or overgrazed soil for egg laying and then moister, grass-covered soil to feed on. Trees help prevent locust build up, as do continuous grass areas. The females drill holes in the hard ground in which to lay eggs. These can stay dormant for up to a year in dry conditions. In summer, eggs are laid deeper so they won't be prematurely hatched by light rain. Often only some of the eggs will hatch: a safeguard against premature hatching if the rain doesn't keep up. Eggs hatch only after rain, sometimes as soon as seventeen days after laying. The adults can mate again in twelve days, with the rain stimulating egg production, with more eggs hatching after seventeen days.

Plague locusts migrate in swams during the day and individually at night, usually following the wind direction, sometimes stopping to continue breeding. They often travel large distances during weather depressions, laying eggs in dry soil. These eggs will emerge after rain when grass is growing.

Plague grasshoppers

Plague grasshoppers, unlike plague locusts, breed only once a year and migrate only a few kilometres.

Controlling grasshoppers and locusts

Locusts and grasshoppers eat leaves. A swarm of plague locusts may be in and out of a garden in a couple of days, and leave it completely defoliated. Conventional gardening and farming advice is to spray any of the grasshopper/locust pests with a 0.1 Maldison spray. Like most conventional pest-control measures this will kill them (and other creatures). It won't control them.

The best long-term control of any pest problem is to eliminate the causes of the plague by redesigning farming or gardening systems or by encouraging predators. Poisonous sprays will wipe out predators without inflicting much long-term harm on the pest.

Predators and parasites

There are three ways to reduce the damage to your plants from grasshoppers and locusts. The first is long term: encourage the birds (especially the straw-necked ibis) that prey on them. One of the best ways to encourage ibis is not to drain swampy 'unproductive' bits of paddock or to build dams with shallow edges. Praying mantids are also predators of grasshoppers, and at least three sorts of wasp, including the egg parasite *Scelio fulgidus* wasps, parasitise locust swarms and may even follow the swarms about. Several wasps also prey on the nymphs. Various fungus diseases also affect locusts and grasshoppers. Tree planting (or avoiding tree clearing) will also encourage birds and reduce grasshopper numbers.

Garden design

Grasshoppers and locusts in plague proportions generally pass through an area, eating both greenery and dry grass. The more greenery around your garden the more it will be protected. In several plagues in our area the gardens surrounded by bush or native hedges were attacked but not devastated, while gardens surrounded by bare paddocks were wiped out. I found that strongly scented plants (such as lavender and callistemons) were mostly avoided by the grasshoppers, and nearby plants also had a degree of protection.

Long-term control

The best control would be long-term control, and unlikely to happen. That is to abandon large-scale, dry grassland farming and scrub clearing; to stop draining wetlands and establish more protected wet areas to breed ibis and other birds (one marsh per paddock should control them); stop using pesticides that wipe out predators. But spraying is easier (in the short term), and spraying will continue while the habits that cause the plagues go unchanged. Locust plagues are white-settler introduced.

Deterrents

Deterrents are just that: they will deter a pest, but not stop it. No deterrent will completely protect anything during a severe plague, when even washing can be eaten from the line, but deterrents may at least prevent your garden from being completely destroyed. Such deterrents may prevent damage altogether where numbers are small. The best grasshopper deterrent is sprays of water, for they dislike flying through them. I protected young citrus trees one year by punching holes in the line that fed the drip irrigation system. Each young tree was protected by a fine spurt of water. Try perforated hoses around the perimeter of the garden for short periods, but be careful not to saturate the soil. Turn the water off at dusk and catch slow moving grasshoppers in the early morning.

Rows of marigolds, larkspurs, pyrethrum, lobelia, tomatoes or rhubarb are supposed to deter locusts and grasshoppers. Plants with tough, strongly scented foliage also appear to deter grass-hoppers. I've found that in bad plagues grasshoppers will eat these too, although they avoid them in good seasons.

Grasshopper repellent

This works for mild invasions: large numbers will ignore it. Grind four chillies, one capsicum and an onion; add four cups of water. Leave for 24 hours. Strain and spray every couple of days.

Traps

Traps can kill large numbers of grasshoppers and locusts. Feed the bodies to the chooks, or compost them. Grasshoppers and locusts are also edible, but not worth the trouble. For a large-scale trap, float pieces of yellow plastic in a children's inflatable swimming pool or any other large body of water. The locust will jump onto the plastic and drown.

Small traps can be made by filling old paint tins or wide-mouthed jars with a 10 per cent molasses solution. Cover with a film of oil to deter bees and mosquitoes. Place as many as possible round the crops you want to protect.

Grasshoppers can also be vacuumed from the air and from sturdy shrubs. Make sure the bag is sealed when you dispose of them. Feed the residue to chooks or compost them.

Chooks and other birds

Chooks eat a lot of grasshoppers. During one mild plague we let chooks free-range in our garden in the early morning when the locusts were still lethargic, and at dusk when the locusts were slowing down and the chooks full of green stuff and unlikely to attack the lettuce. Our garden was almost untouched, while one down the hill was almost wiped out. The chooks turned into white leghorn acrobats, performing great standing leaps and chasing persistent grasshoppers around the hill.

Most large birds catch grasshoppers, especially when there are a lot of them. Even magpies, currawongs, kookaburras and owls change their diet with an abundance of grasshopper food. The more birds you have in your garden, the fewer pests you'll have, including grasshoppers.

Catch them yourself

My father gets up at dawn, when the grasshoppers are lethargic, puts on a pair of gloves and runs his hands over any plant the grasshoppers are damaging. He squashes any grasshopper he finds. He says this puts him in a good frame of mind to cope with the business world later in the day.

Sprays

If you must spray, use a spray that breaks down quickly. Nicotine spray and tomato leaf spray are effective, but will also kill predators who eat the dead grasshoppers. Don't try and spray the grasshoppers themselves. Spray the leaves they'll eat instead. The spray should be ingested for greatest effectiveness.

Possums

Possums used to be a problem in our area, until the powerful owls moved in to control them. But powerful owls need a five-square-mile territory, and this isn't possible in most areas.

You have two choices with possums. You can either put up with them or remove them. The latter will probably mean their death. Possums are very territorial, and will trek for kilometres to get back home. And other possums will kill them or let them starve before they let them stay in their area. Remember that a resident pair of possums will keep out strange possums: and at least you will know your residents' habits.

If you choose to put up with your possums, try feeding them regularly with sweet things, such as apples. They will be less inclined to go for your rosebuds. You could also try other deterrents, just to keep them off new growth. Try cayenne pepper or bitter aloes or spray the plants with *fresh* urine (stale urine will burn the foliage). You could also try netting shrubs when they have a lot of new growth.

Suburban possums mostly live in roofs. Net in your eaves so they can't settle.

Rabbits

You have two choices with rabbits in your garden: you can fence them out or you can kill them. Rabbit repellents work, but only for a short time. They are only a respite while you work out another solution. In the orchard it is another matter. There are several techniques you can use to stop rabbits ringbarking trees. But nothing will stop for long a rabbit nibbling your carrot tips.

Predators

The best here are wedgetail eagles for about 40 per cent of their diet is rabbits. Powerful owls take a good many too. Foxes eat the odd rabbit, but they prefer frogs and small marsupials in our area. I have seen large copperhead snakes eat small rabbits, and cats will also go down rabbit burrows and catch the young. In spite of the fact that we have country that is supposed to be especially suited to rabbits (lots of rough 'scrub' and bushes for them to hide and burrow under) we have fewer rabbits than surrounding, bare farms, probably because we have more things to eat them. Rabbits taste good.

Rabbit-proof fences

A rabbit-proof fence should be of chicken wire, at least a metre high and buried 15 cm deep. Or leave a 15 cm 'skirt' above ground, weighed down by heavy rocks. If the wombats start pushing through the fence, make gates for them: heavy gates on hinges, which a wombat can barrel through, but will be too heavy for a rabbit (who have less initiatve than wombats anyway).

Low-level electric fences will keep rabbits out, but rabbits are stupid. If the electricity is turned off they'll forget about the shock when it was on, and barge through.

I have also made a garden in piles of old car tyres in rabbit infested areas. These were too high for the rabbits to get into easily, and I think the smell was also a deterrent. Anyway, they left them alone.

Rabbits in orchards

We had problems with rabbits ringbarking young trees. The best solution was to put old car tyres around them. This not only kept down the rabbits, but acted as a long-term mulch, keeping in moisture and reducing weeds. The only problem is that you have to remember to remove the tyres before the trees get too big. Cutting a tyre in half is hard work.

Old aluminium foil or tarpaper tied around the base of the tree also stops rabbits. Tie them on with string, which should rot in a year or so and won't ringbark the tree as it gets bigger.

Old tin cans opened at the side and jammed over the trunk work too, but they can ringbark the tree if left on too long and the moist dark space inside the can seems to encourage fungal and bacterial diseases.

Deterrents

There are a range of rabbit deterrents that work as long as the rabbits aren't starving. No deterrent will work if there's nothing much else to eat. Try wood ash or cayenne pepper sprinkled on foliage for a short-term solution (i.e. until it rains, or you want to water, or the wind blows them off).

Human hair in old pantyhose is supposed to keep off rabbits. I have had conflicting results with it. It may depend on how adventurous your rabbits are. Lion dung is supposed to be a foolproof rabbit repellent. First find your lions.

The smell of blood and bone and human urine also make plants less attractive to rabbits, but, again, these work only if there is plenty of choice of other food for the rabbit. A bitter aloe spray (the stuff you buy at chemists to stop kids biting their fingernails) or quassia spray are more effective deterrents.

The following is a rabbit repellent that does work and won't wash off. It is a lot of work to make though, and if you are prepared to go to the trouble of making it, you're probably better off spending your time on fencing.

Dissolve 3 kg powdered resin in 4 litres denatured alcohol (not wood or methyl alcohol, which won't dissolve the resin). Place the alcohol and resin in an airtight container and shake, then leave for a day or two. *Don't* apply heat. Make sure no water gets into the solution. Only prepare as much as you need. It doesn't keep well. Paint it round the bark at the base of your trees. The repellent won't wash off, although rain may turn it white. It should work for about a year. Only use it on bark. It will burn foliage.

You can get resin at ballet supply shops and music shops. There must be other sources. Resin is only dried gum, so you could try experimenting with wattle gum. Alcohol is more difficult to get if you're not a doctor or chemist. Try taking the resin to your local chemist and getting the chemist to mix it up for you.

Slugs and snails

We have one bad burst of snail and slug damage here, in early spring, while the lizards are still snoozing and before the kookaburras discover where they are. We see the odd snail at other times, and crunch a lot on wet nights, but the damage is never severe enough to have to do anything about it.

The best way to keep your slug and snail population under control is to have large numbers of lizards and birds. From the kitchen window I've watched a kookaburra crack and eat six snails in half an hour. Frogs and toads also eat a considerable number. Encourage kookaburras, lizards and frogs, and your slug and snail problem should gradually fade away, except in early spring. Other anti-slug and snail measures include the following.

Garden design

It is possible to design a garden to minimise slug and snail damage. Firstly, make sure your plants are healthy. Sappy nitrogen-fed growth is more likely to attact slug and snail damage. (If you doubt this, grow two cabbages close together. Feed one with compost, one with sulphate of ammonia, and see which one gets eaten.)

Clean up patches of grass and weeds that offer shelter. I found I stopped snail damage on the cabbages by moving the slow 'compost heap' (in reality just a pile of weeds) away.

Deterrents

• Mulch the garden with oak leaves. Even when oak leaves are partially decomposed, snails will avoid them.
• Water with wormwood spray or Bordeaux. Both will repel slugs and snails, but wormwood spray is preferable. Bordeaux can deposit too much copper in the soil and will kill ladybirds and other predators.
• Try any irritating, barrier-slaked lime, crushed eggshells, diatomite, dry wood ash, finely chopped human hair. Spread sharp grit, broken shells.
• Salt is the most effective barrier, but is toxic in your garden. Buy half-inch black polythene pipe, cut out the top third, fill it with

salt, seal off the ends by tying them with wire, then drape the pipe around your garden as a snail fence. Snails won't cross it, and it is easily moved. Be careful it doesn't overflow in the rain.
• Try an electric snail fence with fuse wire and a Big Jim torch battery and icecream sticks. Don't laugh. It works. It should be about 2 mm above the ground.

Snail fences
Edge your garden with a barrier of thin metal, about 40 cm high, with a downwards pointing edge angled outwards. The snails will shelter under the ledge so you can destroy them, and won't be able to climb over it into your garden. A cheaper solution is to take tin cans with tops and bottoms cut out. Press them into the soil so they stand shoulder to shoulder in a long line. Surround your garden with them.

Copper barriers
Slugs and snails won't cross copper. Either surround your garden with a band of copper, or wrap narrow bands round susceptible plants such as cabbages. These can be removed and used again.

Snail soup
Catch your snails on wet nights with the aid of a torch. Crush them. Throw them into a bucket of water. Put the lid on. Leave for a few weeks. Feed the resulting liquid and sludge to your plants. It will be high in calcium, nitrogen and phosphorus, and just possibly a disease carrier or deterrent for other snails.

Traps
Many people try snail traps with no success. They simply haven't used the right bait for their area. Snails are conservative feeders. They will be attracted to similar foods as the ones they are used to. So try several baits until you find one your local population finds palatable.
• Hollowed out raw potatoes.
• Grapefruit or orange halves squeezed out for juice.
• Empty beer cans. Leave them in the garden overnight, throw them in the rubbish next morning full of snails or slugs (very effective).
• Cans filled with bran or wheatgerm.
• A wilted cabbage leaf smeared with dripping.

A non-emptying trap

Fill an icecream container with water. Scatter on a thick layer of bran. Leave mostly submerged in the garden. The snails will crawl up, in and drown; that is, if they like bran.

Ducks and chooks

Some ducks may be left in the garden most of the time to hunt snails, but they have to be trained for it. Otherwise just leave them in for a short time each day. Use active ducks, such as khaki campbells or Indian runners. Give them constant access to green stuff, but give them concentrates only after a hard day's snail clearing. Buy them young or fully trained. Don't give them constant access to deep water where they can swim or they'll forage there instead of your garden.

Try letting hens into the garden for the last hour before they perch. By then they should have had enough green stuff and will eat the slugs and snails without tearing up the garden. This works only with free-range hens. Confined chooks, unless they have been given a lot of greens, will tear into your vegetables without a thought for the snails.

CHAPTER 6

Organic Pesticides and Fungicides

Homegrown pest and disease control

This chapter describes organic alternatives to commercial pesticides and fungicides, remedies that break down quickly and harmlessly, with the least possible harm to the environment, including humans.

There is no need to buy ingredients to treat fungal, bacterial or pest problems in your garden. Those that can't be cured by good management, or tolerated, can be treated or prevented with homegrown ingredients.

More than any other crop, pesticides should be homegrown and homemade. That way you know what you are getting, and the effort of growing and making your own is a disincentive to spraying whenever a bug pops into view. In addition, you will no longer be supporting the chemical multinationals or helping to create Bhopal-like situations, where Third World countries suffer for our pesticide 'needs'.

When to use pesticides

- When you are converting to an organic garden and your plants are vulnerable.
- When numbers build up so they may kill the plant.
- From financial necessity. For example, apples cosmetically damaged by the apple dimpling bug may be wonderful but unsaleable.

But remember that using pesticides costs more in the long run than prevention.
- When you are legally obliged to (as for fruit fly).
- To control a new pest in your area that you don't want to spread.
- Where an introduced pest has few natural predators (such as fruit fly).
- When seasonal or other conditions (such as large-scale spraying in your area or a long, cool, damp spring) produce an unusual build up of pests.

How to use pesticides

Pesticides should always be the last resort. Even organic pesticides, which are made from natural ingredients and break down quickly and harmlessly, may kill useful predators, or at best reduce their food supply so you no longer have them around. Remember that you need some pests to feed the predators, so you will have a naturally stable garden.
- Try mechanical methods first. Pick off pests by hand, use a strong hose, dust off with a paint brush (aphids especially).
- Try traps. For example, cardboard wrapped round trees to trap codling moth; port wine or pheromone lures; light traps (these mostly suppress egg laying); yellow painted boards; aphid traps made from shallow pans of water with yellow colouring and detergent; molasses and water grasshopper traps.
- Try ant barriers for aphids; cutworm trenches filled with derris-impregnated straw; wood ash to keep away slugs; nets to keep out birds; mesh screen or pantyhose to keep away codling moth or cabbage white butterflies and moths.
- Try eggshells to confuse cabbage white butterflies, interplanting, reflective mulch for aphids and thrips, green hessian for cabbage white butterflies and cabbage moths.
- Try repellents. Bordeaux will keep away cabbage white butterflies, slugs and snails; garlic spray keeps away aphids and cabbage white butterfly; tansy spray keeps away cabbage white butterflies and cabbage moth; try mint and onion sprays or the chilli spray on p. 129. (To make these sprays, simply pour boiling water over the herbs, let cool and use.)
- Use predator lures, such as pollen scraped on plants to attract hoverflies, lacewings, etc., or marmite or Vegemite sprays.
- As a last resort (and only as a temporary measure) try organic pesticides, ones that are naturally derived, and break down quickly.

What sprays to use

There is no need to identify most of the pests in your garden to control them. All you need is a basic knowledge of the damage they do; that is, their eating habits. Do try and identify your pest if the damage it is causing is so great something must be done about it. Most pest control is simply a matter of management. Once you know your enemy, you may not have to resort to sprays.

Borers

Damage done   Shoots and even branches may die back. Look for holes and sawdust deposits.

Control   Poke out borers with wire. Plug up holes. Inject derris or pyrethrum.

Fungal and bacterial problems

Damage done   Leaf spots or blemishes. Fruit rots.

Control   Bordeaux on old tough foliage (not blossom or new shoots) or dormant trees; chamomile, elder, chive or horseradish sprays; seaweed, casuarina or horsetail sprays as preventative.

Some pest-like symptoms are not caused by pests at all.

Leaf-eaters

Common pests   Earwigs, grasshoppers, caterpillars, leaf-eating ladybirds.

Damage done   Holes in leaves, ragged leaves, large green droppings.

Control   Encourage birds; pick off by hand or hose off; sprinkle on dried wood ash, diatomaceous earth or lime (be careful not to overlime the soil); try Bordeaux or other repellent sprays; use wormwood, tomato leaf sprays or bug juice. As a last resort use derris spray (spray underneath the leaves as well) or pyrethrum.

Nutritional problems

Symptoms   Foliage yellows, either young or old leaves or between veins. Plants are stunted, crops are small and may drop off before maturity.

Correction   The best food for plants is the residues of whatever has lived before: plant and animal matter. Compost and mulch should be all the feeding plants need. If in doubt, give plants a daily dose of liquid foliar fertiliser for a couple of weeks. If this improves your plants, keep doing it, once a week or fortnight (depending on how strongly your plants are growing) while you correct your feeding programme.

Root-rots

Damage done   Plants yellow or die back suddenly, usually from the top. Plants will rock unsteadily when you shake them.

Control   Cut back tree as a temporary measure and feed with foliar spray while you mulch with compost and correct drainage. You may prefer to dig out the tree to stop the rot spreading to other plants.

Sap-suckers

Common pests   Aphids, bugs, cicadas, scale, thrips, mites, leaf-hoppers.

Damage done   Skeletonised foliage; foliage brown or curled at the edges; leaves appear mottled or pitted. Sap-suckers may also damage new shoots: shoots wilt and die off suddenly. Sap-suckers excrete a lot of sugary wastes, which can promote sooty mould.

Control   Encourage birds and other predators; oil sprays in cool weather; soap sprays; try rhubarb, garlic, nettle, quassia, derris or wormwood sprays.

Other symptoms

Leaf fall   Before you bother about root-rots, check that the plant isn't waterlogged or starved of water, has been adequately fed, isn't being overshadowed by a taller tree or bush. One of the most common questions I have from Canberra people is, 'Why has my lemon tree lost its leaves?' The usual answer is 'Cold temperatures'. Cold-stressed plants don't always look black and frost-bitten. Cold, injured citrus may simply turn listless, yellow and finally defoliate.

No fruit   Young trees may not set fruit, or it may fall off before it is ripe. Frost can destroy blossom so it falls before fruit set, or young fruit can be damaged by frost or hail. Try to remember if there was frost, strong wind or hail at blossoming time. Brown rot can also damage blossom so it fails to set (see page 65).

Many fruit trees need a pollinator to set fruit. Even if your apple tree has fruited by itself for years, the neighbouring pollinator (perhaps several houses away) may have been cut down recently. Result: no fruit on your tree. Poor pollination may result in no fruit setting or premature fruit drop. Cut open a fallen fruit. If it has no or few seeds or misshapen seeds, there is probably a pollination problem. Plant flowers and flowering shrubs to attract bees to your garden at the time your tree flowers.

Codling moth and fruit fly larvae both head for the centre of fruit and damage the seeds. The fruit then falls prematurely (see pages 43-49).

Dieback   This can be caused by insect attack. See if the leaf edges are ragged or the stems chewn. It can be caused by root-rots (try to rock the tree). It may be caused by borers (look for holes and sawdust deposits). It may also be caused by sap-suckers (see if the young shoots are dying back first). Sometimes dieback from sap-suckers on new shoots will spread as a pathogen enters the inury.

Yellowing leaves   If the oldest leaves are yellowing, and not the young ones, you have a nitrogen deficiency. If the young leaves are yellow, you may have a phosphorus deficiency. If all leaves seem to be yellowing evenly, check that the plant isn't waterlogged or starved of water. Plants need water to transfer their nutrients. Rock the plant to see if it seems loose: this would mean root-rot. Cold weather will cause leaves to turn yellow. So will herbicide drift. Check the base of the plant for collar rot or injury from a motor mower.

Failure to grow   Even with the best of treatment, plants that have been badly treated in the past may take several years to start to grow again. We had several apparently dormant trees in the orchard, which had been badly eaten by sheep for several years. It took three years for them to start to grow again, and then they thrived. But if a new tree isn't growing, always check for root-rot. You may have imported it with the tree. Root-rots are best dug out before they spread.

Otherwise check that plants are adequately fed (if they are kept well mulched there isn't much doubt of it) and watered, and are not suffering from competition with grass or larger plants. Old gardens and orchards may suffer from 'replant disease': new plants grown where old ones have been often don't thrive, possibly due to a gradual build up of soil pathogens and soil deficiencies to which the old ones have gradually become tolerant. But, again, a gradual build up in soil condition from mulch and compost will eventually solve the problem.

Plants grown in areas that are too cold or too hot won't thrive either. Shading pergolas, ice on the roots, hessian shelters, etc. may partially solve the heat problem, but in most cases the extra effort won't be worth the trouble. There are so many species available in Australia now, for cold, temperate and tropical climates, that is it is more sensible to keep to your climatic limitations.

Look for scale, as scale inject substances that stop plants growing.

A plant may also be stunted by leaking gas mains. Sniff in still weather.

How to check a plant for pests

Always look under leaves as well as on top; examine the trunk just below soil level as well as above it; breathe on flower petals so thrips move.

How to use organic remedies

• When spraying many trees or plants, always spray every second plant, or every second row, and then spray the rest a week later. This will ensure surviving pests and predators while still cutting down the numbers damaging your plants.

• All organic pesticides break down quickly, often on contact with light. Most are no longer effective after two days or less. This means they must be re-applied if the pests are still in great enough numbers to cause damage.

Organic pesticides must be combined with prevention. Many people claim their organic remedies haven't worked because a week later there are still pests on the plants. The pesticides have worked, but the plants were re-infested. Never use a pesticide without trying to work out the cause of the pest problem.

Most organic pesticides are not harmful. Some, indeed, such as parsnip, turnip or nettle spray, can be turned into a quite good soup. On the other hand some are extremely poisonous. *Always assume any pesticide is poisonous. Label poison. Do not store if possible. Keep out of the reach of children.*

Don't use the family stew pot to make up these recipes. Don't inhale fumes. Always wear gloves and long sleeves when spraying, and preferably a spray mask as well. While the pesticide may not be poisonous, it may very well be irritating. For example, many people are sensitive to the aphid killer wormwood, or to stinking roger or tansy.

The ingredients for most of the following recipes can mostly be bought at grocery and health food stores. I prefer to grow my own ingredients (it is cheaper and easier) just as I prefer to make my own pesticides. If you have to go to the trouble of growing and making your pesticides you won't be tempted to use them indiscriminately. And you'll always know what is in them.

Soap (not detergent) can be added to all recipes as a 'sticking' agent, but sprays will keep better without it.

General pesticides

Bordeaux spray   See fungicides for recipes. This is effective against scale and, to a lesser extent, mites.

Bug juice   Try this on any pest. Success will be variable, but it can be so effective that you will need no other remedy.

Take one part pest, add three parts water. Blend. Leave in a warm, not hot, place for 24 hours. Strain. Dilute with 50 parts water.

Bug juice may work because of pathogens or parasites on the pests, which you are spreading, or because the odour is unpleasant to the other pests.

Buttermilk spray   Use for red spider mites and other mites, as well as their eggs.

Take ½ cup of buttermilk, 4 cups flour, 10 litres water. Spray every two days, under as well as on top of foliage.

Chilli spray   This can be used against caterpillars.

Blend 1 cup dried chillies or 2 cups fresh chillies with 2 cups water. Spray fresh.

Christmas rose (Helleborus niger)   The roots and leaves of this can be dried, ground and used as an insecticide. It can be used where derris would be used, and is reputed to be about the same strength. It is traditionally used for leaf-eating insects.

Clay spray   This will suffocate aphids, thrips and mites. It will also work for scale, but make sure you use clay, not soil, or you may make your scale problem worse. Dilute the clay with enough water to make it sprayable. Be careful not to spray on predators such as ladybird larvae, as it will kill them too.

Coriander spray   This is effective against red spider mites and woolly aphids. Boil one part coriander leaves in one part water for ten minutes. Strain and spray. This can also be used with anise. Alternatively mix four parts of coriander oil in 100 parts soapy water. Shake well until mixed.

Daisy cress (Spilanthes paniculata)   Get hold of this if you can, as an alternative to pyrethrum. It is an annual wild daisy, native to Australia (found only in Queensland) as well as other countries. Its leaves are opposite, its flowers long-stemmed, conical and pungent.

Daisy cress contains spilanthol, a powerful insecticide. It is very effective as a fly spray and mosquito spray, including a spray for mosquito larvae. It is also an anaesthetic.

Derris spray   This is an effective general insecticide, effective on any leaf-eater, such as caterpillars, pear and cherry slug, sap-suckers such as aphids, most weevils, spitfires and fleas. It is usually sold as a dust. It causes minimal harm to humans, but will kill fish (including goldfish in the garden), tadpoles, frogs and toads. It also kills various ladybird larvae, though not hoverfly larvae or bees.

Derris breaks down under sunlight in a few days, so is longer-lasting than pyrethrum. It is not an effective contact poison. It works best when eaten, so is most effective on leaf-eaters.

To make derris powder, dry and then pulverise the root. Derris powder is most conveniently made into a spray. Mix 120 g soap in 4.5 litres water. Add 60 g derris powder mixed in another 4.5 litres water. Dilute with another 2 litres, mix again and spray. This may separate out and need remixing.

A simpler recipe is: mix 1 kg derris powder with 1 kg pure soap powder. Mix with 20 litres of water.

Cultivation   Derris is a natural alkaloid found in the roots of *Derris ellipta* and other derris species. *Derris trifoliata* is a native Australian derris, growing in North Queensland. It is not the source of commercial derris, being much weaker, but can be used in a higher concentration. It is a vigorous rainforest creeper and climber, commonly growing near the shore, with trifoliate or pinnate leaves and flat kidney-shaped pods 3-5 cm long. Derris grows from seed, but I know of no commercial source. It is frost sensitive, and needs deep, good soil and moisture.

Diatomaceous earth spray   Use this against any soft-bodied pest, such as aphids, thrips, mites, snails, termites, or against hard-shelled ones, such as bugs. The fine dust should penetrate their carapaces and gradually wear them away. Spray once every two weeks. It will take that long for the spray to have any effect on bugs.

Mix 200 g diatomaceous earth (the ground skeletons of marine organisms) with 1 litre soapy water.

Dipel (Bacillus thuringiensis)   This is a biological control, a form of germ warfare. It was naturally a silkworm disease in Japan and a disease of wax moth larvae. It needs to be eaten to be effective. The spores are killed by sunlight and must be re-applied once a week. Make sure you spray under the leaves as well as on top.

Dipel is effective on all moth or butterfly caterpillars. It is not supposed to work on sawfly larvae (pear and cherry slug) but is sometimes effective. The infected caterpillars can be eaten by birds or any other predator. There have been no reports of caterpillar resistance to Dipel in Australia, although there have been rumours of this overseas.

You can use Dipel to make your own culture. Gather a cup full of caterpillars from an area that has been sprayed with Dipel four days earlier. Mash them up and add them to three cups of milk warmed to blood heat, so it is neither hot or cold when you dip your finger in. Cover and leave in a warm (not hot) place for three days. Strain, add eight times the amount of water, and spray. A little of the milk mixture can be saved as a starter for the next lot, or gather more infected caterpillars.

Elder spray   This is a general pest-killer, particularly effective on aphids and caterpillars. It is also poisonous to humans and hoverfly larvae, although it appears to spare adult hoverflies, bees, ladybirds and ladybird larvae and most wasps.

Take 500 g elder leaves and smooth-barked stems and cover with 3.5 litres water. Boil, simmer for 30 minutes, topping up as the water boils away. Strain and use undiluted. Elder spray will keep for three months in a sealed container in a dark, cool place, but keep out of the reach of children, and label POISON. Elder spray can also be used as a fungicide.

Eucalyptus oil   Like other oils, eucalyptus oil kills scale, aphids, etc. It should be used only in cool weather, or it may damage young leaves and flowers. Eucalyptus oil will also repel many pests.

Some eucalypts produce far more oil than others. Around here the narrow-leafed peppermint is most favoured for oil production, although any eucalypt can be used at a pinch. Test the oil content by crushing a leaf and smelling or looking for the tiny oil globules on the leaf.

Small quantities of oil can be distilled by simply boiling the leaves in a large pot (not one you will want soon for cooking) *with the lid on.* If the lid is off, the oil will evaporate. Boil the leaves for about an hour, then let them cool, still with the lid on. When they are quite cold, scoop the oil off the top with a teaspoon, gravy strainer or piece of blotting paper.

For a weaker oil, crush the leaves, place them in a saucepan, just cover with bland oil and heat gently *without boiling* for up to an hour. Leave to cool, strain and use. Different eucalypts require different soils. Ask at your local nursery for trees to suit your purpose.

Feverfew   Feverfew is often incorrectly known as 'pyrethrum'. The mistake probably doesn't matter since feverfew can be used exactly like pyrethrum, with the same effect, but double the quantity of flowers must be used.

Flour   Flour is a stomach poison for caterpillars. They eat it and die.

Garlic spray   Garlic spray can be used as a general insecticide in a wide range of situations, but its effect is variable: very effective sometimes, not at all at others. Possibly harsh, arid conditions make it less effective.

However, it is worth trying. Remember it is not a contact poison, and must be eaten to be effective.

Chop 85 g garlic. Don't bother to peel it. Soak in 2 tablespoons mineral oil for 24 hours. Add 600 ml water in which 7 g soap has been dissolved (or as soapy a solution as you can make). Strain and store in glass, not metal, away from light. Dilute with ten times the amount of water to begin with; then make it stronger if it isn't effective.

The smell isn't as bad as you would expect and doesn't linger when sprayed.

Glue spray   This will dry on small pests, suffocating them. Use on aphids, scale, mites, pear and cherry slug, thrips. Spray every five to seven days. It is no use in wet weather.

Take a cup of glue, dissolve in three cups of warm water. Some glues are denser than others: you may need more water. A flour and water paste, homemade, can also be used.

Insect repellent spray   Blend together a mixture of garlic, onion, lavender leaves or flowers, mints, yarrow with just enough water to ensure even blending. Let stand for 24 hours at room temperature in a closed container. Filter, add a few drops of detergent to help sticking, add an equal quantity of water and spray onto plants.

Lantana spray   This is effective against aphids. Boil 500 g leaves in 1 litre water. Strain and spray.

Lantana is a well-known and troublesome weed. If you intend to plant an aphid control, use something else; wormwood, for example. But if you do have lantana, you may as well make use of it.

Marigold spray   Cover marigold flowers with boiling soapy water, leave overnight, strain and spray. Use on aphids.

Mustard seed spray   This kills scale. Mix powdered mustard seed with enough water to make a sprayable mixture. Most powdered table mustard is mixed with flour and turmeric. This can be used at a pinch, but of course won't be as strong as powdered pure mustard.

Neem tree dust   The leaves can be dried and used as a repellent, or they can be ground to a powder to make a general insecticide. Traditionally, this was used to keep weevils away from food.

Cultivation   This is an Asian tree, evergreen, fast-growing, suitable for poor soils and a temperate to tropical climate. It is not frost-tolerant.

Oil spray   Oil sprays work by covering insects or their eggs with a light film of suffocating oil, especially in winter, when the outsides are more porous. Oil sprays cause leaf damage over about 24°C.

Take 1 kg soap for every 8 litres oil. Boil and stir vigorously till it dissolves. Dilute with 20 times the volume of water. This spray separates quickly, so don't store it after it has been mixed with water.

Onion spray (1)   This is good for scale, thrips, aphids and mites.

Pour 500 ml boiling water over 1 kg chopped, unpeeled onions and strain. Dilute with 20 litres of water. Spray every ten days until pests are gone.

Pepper   Dust white or black pepper over caterpillars.

Powdered sulphur   This is an old-fashioned mite remedy, which also kills predators. It should not be used in hot weather as plants may burn. Ask for powdered sulphur or flowers of sulphur at hardware stores or chemists.

Pyrethrum spray   Pyrethrum is a broad spectrum spray. It is worth trying on any pests. It will kill some predators, but has a low toxicity for humans and animals. It breaks down in sunlight, from two hours to two days. Spray it at night outdoors so it doesn't affect bees and other useful species. Pyrethrum has about a 12-hour toxicity.

Pick the flowers before they are fully open for the best effect. The flowers can be dried on sheets of newspapers in a well-ventilated place, then pulverised into a powder and mixed with water for spraying, or pulverised for flea powders and other insecticide powders, or made into 'tea' for pyrethrum spray.

The active ingredients in pyrethrum are not soluble in water, though you will get some insecticide effect by covering 1 tablespoon of dust or 2 tablespoons of flowers with 1 litre of hot soapy water for an hour. However, you will get far better results if you just cover the pyrethrum with any alcohol (like brandy or sherry), or with light mineral oil. Kerosene can also be used, but it is not a safe ingredient for use as a fly spray or on tender plants. Leave the pyrethrum to soak overnight, and then add the hot soapy water as above, and leave for an hour. Strain and spray. Never boil pyrethrum spray—the fumes can be toxic—and don't stand the spray in direct sunlight. Home-made pyrethrum spray can be kept for a few days only in a cool and very dark place.

Cultivation   Pyrethrum spray is not made from your common garden white daisy-like pyrethrum flowers, but from the flowers of dalmation pyrethrum, *Tanacetum cinerariifolium*. A few have begun to appear in nurseries in the last few years, and seed is available from Phoenix Seeds (PO Box 9, Stanley, Tasmania, 7331) and other nurseries. It is a low-growing plant, to about 80 cm, rather bushy and woody at the base. The lower leaves are alternate and divided into five segments on the flowering stems. The other leaves are smaller and form only two or three segments. There is one flower-head per stalk, with yellow and white flowers, although some ornamental cultivars are also sold. These two have insecticidal qualities, although the quantity of active ingredient may vary, and you may have to make a stronger spray.

Treat pyrethrum like any other chrysanthemum. Let it die down in winter, pick the blooms for use in pyrethrum sprays or leave them to ornament the garden, where they will act as pest repellents next to vulnerable plants such as cabbages. Pyrethrum will also tolerate growing in pots indoors near a well-lit window or on the patio and is fairly drought resistant.

Rhubarb spray   This spray is poisonous. It is also harmless to bees and breaks down quickly.

Boil 1 kg leaves with 3 litres water for 30 minutes. Add enough soap to colour, and dilute with an equal portion of water before spraying. Keep out of the reach of children and label POISON.

Ryania spray   Ryania is a Latin American shrub, native to Trinidad. I don't know a source of ryania shrubs in Australia. This is hard to find ryania powder in Australia and it is usually expensive. Although it is very successful overseas with a wide range of caterpillars and beetles, including codling moth, it is less effective in the hotter, more arid Australian conditions. It is harmless to most but not all common predators.

Mix 1 kg ryania powder with 100 litres soapy water. Spray every ten to fourteen days.

Sacred basil spray (Ocimum sanctum)   Sacred basil looks rather like marjoram. This is native to Australia as well as much of south-east Asia. The fresh, crushed leaves can be rubbed on the skin as a mosquito repellent. Otherwise the leaves can be used in the same way as pyrethrum flowers, although they are not as strong. To make an insecticide from sacred basil, crush the leaves then pour on boiling water. Steep till the tea is a dark brown and use undiluted wherever pyrethrum would be used.

Silverbush spray (Sophora tomentosa)   This has insecticidal properties similar to nicotine. It is a native. Use the leaves as you would tomato leaves to make a silverbush spray.

Soap spray   Try to find soap made with caustic potash, not caustic soda. At least one is available from garden centres. Ordinary soap is far less effective and worse for the soil and plants. Do not use detergents.

Soap spray spares nearly all predators as well as bees, but kills aphids, scale and small caterpillars. Soap spray penetrates into insects' waxy cuticle and kills them. Mix the soap with water until it is milky and frothy. The amount needed will depend on the hardness of your water.

Stinging nettle spray (1)   Cover nettles with water, leave for three weeks or until the liquid is pale brown to green. This can be diluted with two parts water and used for aphids. It is also a valuable foliar fertiliser and an excellent tonic for your plants. Use it freely.

Stinging nettle spray (2)   Boil nettles for 10 minutes in enough water to cover them. Dilute to weak-tea colour, strain and spray. This is effective against aphids and a good foliar spray and fertiliser or general plant tonic.

Sugar spray   Dissolve 2 kg sugar in a bucket of water. Drench the soil to kill nematodes. Molasses can also be used. Don't use honey. It may transmit diseases to bees.

Tomato leaf spray   This is a toxic spray. Do not store. Keep away from children.

Take a quantity of tomato foliage. Cover with water. Bring to the boil. Cool. Use at once. Use as a general insecticide.

Turnip or parsnip spray   Turnip spray kills pea aphids, red spider mites and flies. Parsnip spray kills mites and pea aphids.

Blend roots with just enough water to make this possible, let stand overnight in a sealed container, filter, add equal quantity of water spray. Neither spray is poisonous to humans or animals.

White cedar spray   Crush the leaves or fruit, steep in just enough boiling water to cover them till cool, then spray on pests, from snails to aphids to beetles, and brush through animals' coats to kill and repel fleas. Make a moist poultice of the crushed flowers and apply it to chooks' legs to kill lice.

Cultivation   White cedar (*Melia azedarach*) is an attractive garden tree, native to rainforests, grown in Queensland, Northern Territory and the warmer parts of New South Wales. It has lilac flowers and poisonous yellow fruit. It prefers a deep, moist, but well-drained soil, with plenty of humus and a frost-free spot.

Wormwood spray   This both kills and repels fleas and other pests, such as flies, moths and mosquitoes. It is effective against aphids, deters snails if sprayed around seedlings. Wormwood tea is an excellent insecticide for sap-suckers such as bean, tomato and onion fly and whitefly.

To make wormwood spray, cover chopped leaves with boiling water and leave for three hours. Dilute with one part spray to four of water.

Wormwood is a bitter aromatic herb containing a volatile oil made up of various organic acids and a bitter glucocide, absinthe. The active ingredients come from the leaves and flowerheads. Either can be used, or more traditionally both at once. Pick the leaves and flower stalks just before or during flowering for the best effect, although if needed they can be picked at any time.

Fungal and bacterial conditions

Preventative measures

- Don't introduce the disease. Mildew spores can be spread by wide skirts or brushing trousers; bacterial gummosis can be spread on pruning tools. After three years without curly leaf we introduced it again on young fruit trees.
- Healthy plants, like healthy people, are less susceptible to disease. The less stress (too little or too much water, cold or heat stress, old age, etc.) your plant has, the less disease-prone it will be. This year I had only enough compost for half my silver beet plants. Those that had compost were blemishless throughout winter. The others had withered leaves from leaf spot.
- Try crop rotation if disease is a problem. Most diseases have specific hosts.

• Mulch. This may cover infected material. I deep-mulch fruit trees and roses in winter, covering any diseased leaves. Mulch can also inhibit various pathogens. Verticulum wilt on potatoes or tomatoes, for example, can be inhibited with a barley straw mulch. *Phytophthora cinnamomi* is inhibited by compost, lucerne hay or composted tree bark. And plants with mycorrhizal infection (which needs a stable and rich humus level, see page 12) are less prone to infection.

• Use barrier crops. Some disease spores are carried by wind. Barriers will inhibit their spread.

• Practise rigorous garden hygiene. If you see infected fruit or leaves prune out dead wood and twigs.

• Green manure not only helps crop rotation, some green manures inhibit disease. A soybean green manure, for example, inhibits the build up of potato scab.

• Improve air flow by pruning, thinning fruit or cutting air channels through your garden.

• Use regular liquid green manure, seaweed, nettle, casuarina or horsetail sprays as necessary as preventatives. To make liquid green manure, cover plants (even weeds) with water. Spray on plants when the water is the colour of weak tea.

Fungicides

All-purpose preventative spray   Take as many of the following as possible: nettles, comfrey, chamomile, seaweed, waterweed, lucerne, yarrow, casuarina, horsetail, horseradish leaves. Cover with water. Spray on foliage when the water is a weak-tea colour. Add more water to the plants and use again when strong enough. The remnant can finally be used for mulch.

Baking soda spray   This is not strictly organic. Use instead of Bordeaux. It is slightly easier to make. Never use on foliage.
   Mix 100 g of washing soda with 50 g soft soap. Dilute with 2 litres of water.

Bordeaux mixture   This is the standard organic fungicide. It is very effective against a wide range of parasitic fungi and bacteria. Unlike many modern fungicides, pathogens seem not to develop resistance against it. It sticks very strongly to trees once sprayed, and if it has been made properly and used fresh, even rain shouldn't affect it.
   Always make Bordeaux mixture yourself. It doesn't keep, and commercial mixtures are not traditional Bordeaux. Always use Bordeaux within an hour of making it, or it will start to separate. If it has been let stand

for more than two or three hours it won't stick to the plants, and may injure them. Try not to use Bordeaux too often. Try the other, 'softer' fungicides first. Too much copper can affect soil fungi (high humus levels can mitigate this) and may also kill predators.

If you have trouble with scale in spring and have been spraying with Bordeaux, this may be the reason. Try spraying every second bush, then spraying the rest ten days later, so you still have a nucleus of predators for when pests start to build up.

Bordeaux is made from copper sulphate (bluestone) and calcium hydroxide (hydrated or brickies' lime). Calcium carbonate or agricultural lime (the sort you would normally use in the garden) doesn't work at all. Both can be bought quite easily from hardware stores. Try to get fine crystals of copper sulphate. They dissolve more easily than the coarse ones, which need a lot of stirring.

Make sure the hydrated lime is from an unopened bag. Once the calcium hydroxide is exposed to air it becomes carbonated to calcium carbonate, and won't neutralise the copper sulphate. The resulting spray may severely damage your trees.

Mix 90 g of blue copper sulphate with 6.5 litres of cold water in a non-metallic container: plastic, glass, wood, earthen ware. Never use iron or galvanised iron for Bordeaux. In a second non-metallic container, mix 125 g of slaked lime (brickies' lime, not agricultural lime) in another 2.5 litres cold water in a non-metallic container. If either is lumpy, put it through a strainer. Lime may also be mixed with bits of sand, and unless strained may block the spray nozzle. The copper sulphate must be thoroughly dissolved in sufficient water, or it may form a suspended precipitate that will sink to the bottom and not stick so well to the plants. Mix the two together. Stir well.

Test with an old nail. Dip it in the mixture for thirty seconds. If it comes out blue, you need more lime, or more mixing to dissolve the lime. Don't use it till you have corrected the problem—you may burn your plants.

Use within an hour, stirring occasionally. Use it with any spraying equipment, but have some water around to wash out the nozzles and stop clogging. Bordeaux is used mostly at budswell for deciduous plants, after blossoming for evergreens, and at half-strength on grapes and vegetables through the season for downy mildew. When spraying trees, make sure you spray *all* the bark, including the crutch of the tree.

If your trees are prone to canker or branch dieback, it is a good idea to spray your trees just before pruning. This will make all the remaining leaves drop off. Then spray again after pruning. If leaves drop off after spraying, infection may still enter at the new, uncovered places.

Large-scale measures: for spraying large orchards, the conventional measure is 1 part copper sulphate and 1 part lime to 100 litres of water. This is a slightly stronger recipe than above, but should be made and used in the same way.

Bordeaux paste   This is useful for collar rot and tree wounds. Dissolve 60 g copper sulphate in 2 litres water, then add 120 g of brickies' lime, also mixed in 2 litres of water. 1 tablespoon powdered skim milk can also be added to this mixture to increase its effectiveness.

Casuarina or she-oak spray   Use as for equisetum tea. Make it with 800 g of needles to 1 litre of water.

Chamomile tea   This is a very mild fungicide. Cover a handful of flowers in boiling water, or use a teabag according to instructions on the packet. Spray when cool. It is excellent for damping off (drizzle round seedlings) or for spraying every few days on fruit to ward off brown rot.

Chive tea   Chive tea can be made like chamomile tea, and used for the same purposes. It is especially good against apple scab, but should be sprayed every two weeks in the last months of winter, until just before bud burst.

Condy's crystals   Use this for powdery mildew. Dissolve 7 g potassium permanganate (Condy's crystals) in 7 litres of water. Spray at once.

Garlic spray   See pesticides (p. 131) for the recipe. Garlic spray is an effective fungicide. Unfortunately it also kills insects and should be used with discretion. Use garlic spray for brown rot, curly leaf, fusarium wilt, but other, non-pesticide remedies should be used if possible.

Horseradish spray   This can be used for brown rot and curly leaf. Take a cup of leaves, cover with water, boil for 20 minutes. Add four parts water. Spray at once.

Horsetail or equisetum tea   This is usually a preventative, not a cure. Use it for powdery mildew, curly leaf, brown rot and other fungal and bacterial problems. It does have limited effectiveness, however, when symptoms appear, and if you cut off all infected leaves it may stop the infection spreading. It should be sprayed fortnightly.

Boil 20 g of equisetum leaves (most health food stores have them) with 1 litre of water for 30 minutes. Strain and spray. Use at the rate of 1 litre to cover an area 10 metres by 10 metres for the first spray, then dilute with 50 per cent more water for subsequent sprays. You won't get better control spraying more heavily, as it is a homeopathic spray. If you are growing your own horsetail, the stems and roots are more effective than the leaves.

Kocide   This is a commercially available copper sulphate spray. In trials in my own garden I haven't found it nearly as effective as bordeaux, but others may have different results.

Milk spray   This spray is effective against a range of mildews. Spray equal parts of milk and water every few days until the condition is cleared.

Mustard seed flour   Grind mustard seeds to a fine powder. Dust over plants affected by powdery mildew.

Nettle tea   This can be used against powdery mildew. It is also effective against aphids. Take a container of nettles, cover with water and leave for three weeks or until the water is mid brown. Spray undiluted.

Seaweed spray   This should be sprayed regularly throughout the year at monthly intervals to combat brown rot, curly leaf, black spot and other fungal and bacterial conditions. Spray on foliage at any time of the year. It will also act as a foliar fertiliser and help improve frost resistance.

Wash seaweed if it has been sitting on the beach getting impregnated by the salt from spray. Weed fresh from the sea needs no washing. Cover with water, leave till the water turns pale brown, and spray. Add more water to the residue to re-use. The remaining organic matter can finally be used as an excellent weed free mulch.

Urine   Try this before you reject it. Human urine is very effective against a range of mildews, as well as against apple and pear scab. Urine is sterile unless the donor has a urinary tract infection. It doesn't remain sterile when stored, and will develop a strong odour. Most people find the smell of other people's urine more offensive than their own. If you decide to use it, use it fresh.

Washing soda spray   Use this for downy mildew. Dissolve 110 g washing soda in 5.5 litres of cold water. Add 56 g soft soap. Use at once.

PEST CONTROL CALENDAR

This calendar is designed for temperate areas. Cold and sub-tropical areas may be up to a month earlier or later.

JANUARY

Problems

Apple and pear scab (especially in humid weather), bean fly, black spot, borers, brown rot, budworms in corn, bugs, codling moth, fruit-eating beetles, fruit fly, light-brown apple moth, melon aphids, oriental peach moth, pera and cherry slug, powdery or downy mildew, two-spotted mite or red spider, white fly, wingless grasshoppers, woolly aphids (especially if you've pruned heavily).

Prevention

- Inspect all your fruit for fruit fly and codling moth at least once a week, and pick off any fruit with sting marks or small holes at either end. See lures and baits on pp. 43-51.
- Powdery mildew may affect apples—especially johnnies—as well as vine crops. Use seaweed or casuarina or horsetail tea as a preventative once or twice a fortnight.
- Pick out fruit infected with brown rot. Fruit may have to be thinned. See sprays on pp. 136-39.
- Make sure all fallen fruit is picked up immediately to deter fruit sucking bugs.
- Wingless grasshoppers often become a major pest to trees in January, as grass dies out and they move onto your greenery. See controls on pp. 113-17.
- Prune out foliage affected with powdery or downy mildew; renew mulch to stop spores from spreading; be careful not to transfer spores on skirts or tools.
- Plant new crops of cucumber and zucchini to prolong cropping, in case the first crop is affected by powdery mildew.
- Scatter egg shells to decoy cabbage white butterflies.
- Spray under melon leaves with a strong hose to dislodge melon aphids.
- Plant a bean, pea, oat or wheat crop now, to mature before you plant root crops that might be susceptible to root weevil.

FEBRUARY

Problems

Aphids on cabbages and cauliflowers etc., apple and pear scab, bean fly, black spot, brown rot, bud worms in corn, bugs, cabbage white or cabbage moth caterpillars, codling moth, fruit fly, light-brown apple moth, oriental peach moth, pear and cherry slug, potato moth, sooty mould, 28-spotted ladybird, two-spotted mite or red spider, white fly, woolly aphids.

Prevention

See also January.

- At the first sign of mildewed pumpkin, melon or grape vines, pull off the infected leaves and compost or burn them.
- Stone fruit picked for storage can be treated by dipping them in hot water for about thirty seconds. If their skins shrivel, hold them under for a shorter time: you'll have to vary this according to the heat of the water and the moisture content of the fruit.
- Cabbage white and cabbage moth butterflies may be a problem on young brassica seedlings. In very bad areas, plant seeds later or plant advanced seedlings that have been kept under nets: more mature plants are less vulnerable, and there are fewer pests later in the season. See p. 80.
- This is a good time for summer pruning—especially vines like kiwi fruit— now the fruit has set. Cuts won't be as susceptible to woolly aphids or fungal or bacterial conditions, and will heal faster. A little bending back of unwanted growth will check plants far less than a rigorous pruning in winter. If you must prune apricots or cherries, do so now. Pruning now shouldn't encourage soft growth in autumn, when it would be cut by frost.
- Push in old tin cans as root guards for club root on brassicas.
- Mulch potatoes for potato moth.
- Plant strawberries now around fruit trees to help attract predators against oriental fruit moth.

MARCH

Problems

Apple and pear scab, bacterial blight in walnuts, black spot, brown rot, bugs, codling moth, fruit fly, light-brown apple moth, pear and cherry slug, sawflies, two-spotted mite or red spider, woolly aphids.

Prevention

- Try derris spray against sawflies. Place a bird table and water under affected trees to attract the birds that will control them naturally.
- Don't store apples with codling moth blemishes: the moths will hatch and increase the problem next year. Use any blemished fruit at once, and dispose of any "worms" carefully.
- Check eggplant too; they can be infected by codling moth, and infested plants should be disposed of under water or in sealed bags.
- Keep up fruit fly lures until none have been caught for three weeks.
- Still keep an eye out for red spider, and pear and cherry slug; though most pests will be disappearing as the weather cools down.
- Make sure organic matter in the soil for onions and other root crops is decomposed. DO NOT dig it in.
- Plant flowers to attract predators in spring.
- Plant Chinese cabbage now as a trap crop for spring aphids.

APRIL

This isn't a bad time of the year for pests: the great population explosions have come and gone, and predator numbers should have built up to cope with the remnants.

Problems

Aphids on early broad beans, bacterial canker, black peach aphids, black spot, bugs, codling moth, fruit fly in warm areas, powdery and downy mildew, shot hole.

Prevention

- Prepare for broad bean sowing by adding potash in wood ash, or comfrey, or good compost to the soil. This improves fruit set in both hot and in frosty conditions, and makes the plants much less susceptible to chocolate spot. Make sure you plant the rows with the prevailing wind, to maximise air circulation.
- This is a good time of the year to make compost, not because the compost will move quickly—hot weather means faster compost—but because you'll be pulling out spent crops in the garden for the spring meals of broad beans and peas. Clean up all old or infected material.
- If you have winter-maturing fruit, keep up your fruit fly traps and orchard hygiene. Otherwise, just make sure that you don't have any old fruit in nice, warm, slowly decomposing compost heaps or pits: places where fruit fly can cosily over-winter.
- Check any late-maturing apples like democrats or grannies or Lady Williams every few days for the sawdust-like deposits from codling moth larvae. Remove any old ladders or boxes near the trees where codling moth can hibernate, pick up any windfalls, or let the chooks do it for you.
- Stick some broad pieces of cardboard on the ground around the garden to trap harlequin beetles: check each afternoon for sheltering beetles. This should reduce their number in your garden considerably next season.
- Autumn aphids should be more easily cleaned up by predators than early spring aphids. Collect black parasitised woolly aphids, and keep them safe indoors until spring. Pick off broad bean tips infested with aphids; rinse thoroughly, and steam or boil or stir-fry and eat them: they are very tender, with a mild, spinach-like flavour.
- Plant broad beans where tomatoes are to go in spring, to help prevent verticulum wilt.
- Spray celery with bordeaux against celery spot leaf.

MAY

Problems

Bugs, codling moth, fruit fly in warm areas, leaf spot, wood cankers, woolly aphids or sooty mould on evergreens.

Prevention

This is a month of prevention for next summer.

- Wash off sooty mould with soapy water. This will also help deter the aphids or other sap suckers that are probably causing the mould. Use bordeaux for leaf spots, or just prune them off.

- Prune off dead twigs, look for cankers and prune back to good wood.
- Band apple trees with grease or corrugated cardboard or old wool to help control codling moth and oriental peach moth, and clean up old ladders and fruit boxes where moths may be sheltering. Let hens scavenge around the orchard to pick up old fruit or insects on the ground.
- Many garden catalogues come out around now. Start thinking about ordering pest control plants for next season: wormwood, pyrethrum, helleborus, feverfew, elder, chamomile, horsetail and chives for sprays; strongly scented plants for repellents; flowering annuals and shrubs to attract birds and other insect predators.
- Take lavender cuttings now, and place them in pots that can be moved around the garden. Lavender's scent and shape makes it an excellent deterrent for a range of pests.
- Inspect all apples for storage for signs of codling moth; inspect old fruit boxes, sheds, ladders, etc for cocoons.
- Spray citrus at petal fall with half strength bordeaux for scab and other problems.
- Inspect root vegetables still in the ground for cankers or rotting. If you find any affected, dig them out and leave the hole open to the sun to stop it from spreading.
- Spray any annual seedlings with chamomile tea. Cool moist winter weather may cause a range of fungus problems.
- Place clear plastic over tomato patches for three weeks to clear up any verticulum wilt infection. (Or plant broad beans, or do both.)
- Plaster trees with a cow manure and clay paste for two-spotted mite or red spider and overwintering codling moth cocoons.
- Spray bordeaux at leaf fall for bad cases of curly leaf, brown rot, apple and pear scab, bacterial blight of walnuts, canker, black spot, and mildews.
- Spray with full-strength urine for apple and pear scab, to control the remaining spores in the orchard.
- Spray strawberries with half-strength bordeaux when fruiting stops, for leaf spots and berry rots.
- Clean out green houses now, and leave them open to the sun for a time. Take shelves out to air, and wash them in mild disinfectant if they may be harbouring fungus or disease spores.
- Mow closely under fruit trees or bring animals into the garden to make sure all fallen fruit and other residues are cleaned up.

JUNE

Problems
Bugs, fruit fly in warm areas, leaf spot, onion maggot.

Prevention
This is the time to clean up and plan. See which way the frost flows in your garden, which birds are resident through winter, what spaces you have left to plant and where the sun and shadow lines are in the new winter angles of the sun.

- In most areas there are few outbreaks of pests at this time of year, but you may have overwintering populations, especially of fruit fly and codling moth. Any remaining fruit or windfalls should be rigorously checked to prevent an early build-up of pests when the weather warms.
- If you have apple trees, mark which parsnips you will let go to seed in spring. Parsnips and other umbellifera allowed to spring up wild around the orchard reduce codling moth infestations. Choose some brassicas, especially broccoli, to flower too: flowering brassicas will attract hoverflies and lacewings, and a range of wasps.
- Spray fruit trees, vines, and small fruit with bordeaux against curly leaf, rust, shot hole, brown rot, black leaf spot, bacterial blight in walnuts, and other fungal and bacterial conditions.
- Spray currants with bordeaux for mites. Spray vines with bordeaux for early mites and Rutherglen bugs.
- Rub off loose bark on trees, especially in crotches, to prevent overwintering mites or red spider.
- Clean up slow-composting rubbish: it may harbour slugs, snails, harlequin beetles, etc that will become a problem next spring.
- Spray full-strength urine against apple and pear scab.
- Prune out all dead wood, especially twigs that have died back.
- Pick off shrivelled 'mummies' from fruit trees.
- Place ash between onions to deter onion maggot.

JULY

Problems

Early aphids (black and green), early scale, leaf spots, sooty mould on evergreens, woolly aphids.

Prevention

Finish off the jobs not done last month. Don't leave them any longer, or the new growth may take you by surprise.

- Sooty mould grows where sap suckers have been feeding; try grease banding to control ants. Wipe off the mould with a soapy wettex.
- This is a good time to squash woolly aphids between your fingers: the trees are dormant and the white ovals are easy to see.
- If you have early aphids, try attracting birds: it will be too cold for most other predators. See pp. 38-43.
- Spray trees with home-made oil spray against scale and other overwintering pests. (Do not combine with bordeaux spray and leave at least ten days between sprays.)
- Spray roses with bordeaux or full-strength urine or other fungicides immediately after pruning. (But leave the pruning until next month in cold areas.)
- Place grease bands on fruit trees if they are likely to be infected by red spider or two-spotted mite.
- Renew mulch in the garden and orchard, to cover up infected debris from last season.
- Whippersnip the flowering tops off weeds, to prevent a build-up of thrips and mites in spring.

- Leave land completely fallow for six weeks to cut down cutworm infestations.
- Clean up garden rubbish and make a final winter compost heap.

AUGUST

Problems
Brown rot, curly leaf, pear leaf blister mite, powdery mildew, red spider or two-spotted mite, rust, vine leaf blister mite, woolly aphids.

Prevention
This is the time of soft, sappy growth—high on the menu of most pests!
- If you are worried by outbreaks of pests in spring, try not to water spring crops, and do not fertilise them until the spring flush is over. Try to cut down on soft early growth. Later, more even growth won't be so pest attractive, and by then there'll be more predators around to deal with them.
- Avoid high-nitrogen fertilisers, relying instead on the steady fertility from decaying organic matter in the soil. Do not use any fertiliser in late winter, as there will be an excess of free nitrogen in spring.
- Do not water with large intervals—say, once a week—or when the soil is dry. Keeping moisture content constant through drip irrigation and good mulching is much more effective, and not only in controlling aphids. On the other hand, scale and two-spotted or red spider mite may be reduced with a strong overhead spray. (See chapter 1, A Healthy Garden)
- Let last year's vegetables flower instead of hauling them all out. The adult form of many pest predators will be attracted by the flowers.
- Plant native shrubs for winter flowering (most garden pest predators are natives too), and plant annuals for the mid-summer heat.
- Put out parasitised woolly aphids now; small wasps will hatch and help control the pests in your garden. Try sticking bee pollen onto any plant that you suspect may be pest-prone, to attract predators to it.
- Spray deciduous trees, shrubs and vines again at bud swell with bordeaux or other fungicides, if the previous year has been bad for curly leaf, brown rot, bacterial gummosis, etc.
- Spray with diluted marmite to attract lacewing and hoverfly predators.
- Put out fruit fly lures and check weekly to see if they are flying.
- Renew mulch in the garden and orchard to cover up infected debris from last season.
- Spray blossom with chamomile in wet weather, particularly if brown rot has damaged it before, to improve fruit set.
- Water trees thoroughly overhead if there are thrips in the blossoms. Count the thrips. If there are more than six per blossom, consider spraying to save the fruit crop.
- Spray onions with bordeaux for mildew and onion neck rot.
- Put out slug and snail bait, traps, and fences to protect seedlings and soft, new spring growth.
- Use foil mulches and bug traps at the base of fruit trees against stink and other bugs.

SEPTEMBER

Problems

Aphids, apple and pear scab, apple dimpling bug, bean fly, black spot, brown rot on blossoms and on twigs causing die-back, bugs, carrot fly, chocolate spot on broad beans, codling moth in warm areas, curly leaf, grasshoppers, green vegetable bug, harlequin beetles, leaf spots, mildew, rust, scale, shot hole, sooty mould, thrips, woolly aphids, whitefly, young caterpillars.

Prevention

This is the worst time for aphids: soft new growth and few predators yet. See pp. 38 and 75.

- Thrips may attack blossom now, as winter weeds die off, and the thrips need to look for alternative food supplies. They are particularly attracted to apple blossom. Control winter weeds, and make sure there is an alternative flowering ground cover. See p. 59.
- Woolly aphids may be sucking now too, especially where plants have been too heavily pruned. Consider summer pruning instead (wounds heal faster), and prune only if it is really necessary.
- Spray white oil to control mites or scale or mite eggs if the temperature is below 24°C.
- Plant onions with carrots to deter carrot fly.
- Put out slater, cutworm and earwig baits.
- Tie up black woolly aphids on infected trees.
- Cover the ground with clear plastic for three weeks after brassicas if they have been infected with black cabbage rot.
- Spray fruit with chamomile tea or regular seaweed sprays for brown rot and blossom fall due to curly leaf or brown rot.
- Check fruit fly lures.
- Put out codling moth lures now, or a week before the first codling moth was caught in your trap last year.
- Plant nasturtiums under fruit trees to help control aphids and woolly aphids.
- Spray apples at green tip stage with bordeaux to control scab and bitter rot.

OCTOBER

Problems

Aphids, apple and pear scab, black spot, brown rot, bugs, codling moth, grapevine moth, harlequin beetles, jassids, leaf spot, powdery mildew, shot hole, sooty mould, thrips, and vine leaf blister mite.

Prevention

There should be more predators now the weather is getting warmer: hoverflies and lacewings daring around the blossoms in your garden and clearing up the remnants of the early spring pests.

- If you are pestered by severe outbreaks of scale in spring, look at your general cultivation. Late winter bordeaux sprays, for example, may be the reason, killing off predators. Spray in early winter, or only spray

every second row, finishing off the rest ten days later. See p. 56.
- Sooty mould can be a scale or ant or aphid problem, encouraged by excreted honeydew. Try grease banding the base of the plants, or growing tansy around the trunk to control ants, aphids, brown and black scale, and sooty mould.
- White fly swarm up in clouds if disturbed on carrots and other root crops, ferns, grasses, citrus, and rhododendrons. They are worst in spring and autumn. Try spraying with soapy water (don't use detergent though), or with garlic spray. Add potash to your soil with wood ash or compost or comfrey mulch, so that the problem does not return. Put out yellow-painted boards covered with glue or motor oil to trap white flies.
- When three-quarters of the blossom has fallen, spray apples and pears with diluted urine against apple and pear scab.
- Keep up seaweed sprays for brown rot and general fungal and bacterial problems.
- Let parsnips and other umbellifera go to seed for codling moth control.
- Skirt trees with hessian traps for the fruit tree weevil, which pupates in the branches.
- Strawberries should be sprayed with bordeaux about now against black spot, mildew, and a range of fungi.
- Check for stem borer in currants, and prune off infected branches.
- Keep up codling moth lures and fruit fly traps.
- Keep a good supply of chive or chamomile tea on hand against black spot, scab, mildew, and brown rot. Affected plants may be sprayed every couple of days.
- Mulch strawberries and rhubarb now. Mulching now prevents leaf disease later.
- If brown rot has been a problem in the past, you may need to thin your fruit. Use casuarina, seaweed, or horsetail tea as a preventative.

NOVEMBER

Problems
Aphids, apple and pear scab, bean fly, black spot, brown rot, bugs, codling moth, early pear and cherry slug, freckle, fruit fly, harlequin beetle, oriental fruit moth, oriental peach moth, powdery mildew (especially of vines), rust, and shot hole.

Prevention
- If your peaches have curly leaf, badly infected young trees could be sprayed with a 1-in-10 bordeaux mixture, which will at least save young leaves coming on, and new shoots even if it burns the old foliage. If the condition isn't quite so bad, try spraying with chamomile tea every few days for a couple of weeks. Or just hope that a hot, dry summer will solve the problem for you.
- If brown rot appears, pick off all affected fruit at once, then spray every week with garlic spray or chive tea. Thinning the fruit will let air circulate, which helps reduce brown rot.
- Pear and cherry slug may attack pears, cherries, hawthorns, and sometimes plums, apples, and quinces. Keep the trees growing as strongly as you can to outgrow any damage. For controls, see pp. 53-6.

- 'Red spider' mites get worse during dry periods. Try overhead watering, mulch weeds below the plants, especially capeweed and clover. See pp. 61-2.
- Celery leaf spot can be controlled with bordeaux spray.
- Slugs and snails may attack soft 'forced' plants like lettuce and young seedlings. Predators like frogs and lizards will clean them up later in the year. For traps and baits, see p. 120.
- Downy mildew may first appear now on grapes. Use half strength bordeaux spray to control it.
- Check fruit fly lures and citrus fruit and early fruit like loquats for fruit fly stings.
- Check codling moth lures.
- Paint borer repellent on sickly and old native trees.
- Spray berries with chamomile tea for fungal problems and fruit rots.
- Band trees with hessian for oriental fruit moth and codling moth larvae. Inspect every two days.
- Plant clover now to be a companion crop with brassicas planted in January. Mow the clover and dig a path to plant the seedlings, then let the clover grow flowers when they are finger-high, to help protect against cabbage white butterfly caterpillars.

DECEMBER

Problems

Aphids, apple and pear scab, black spot, borers, brown rot, bugs, Christmas and other beetles, codling moth, fruit fly, light-brown apple moth, oriental peach moth, pear and cherry slug, powdery mildew, stem borer in currants, two-spotted mite or red spider, white fly, wingless grasshoppers.

Prevention

- December brings mildews and fruit rots and other problems of humidity. Thin out fruit if necessary, to help control brown rot; avoid transferring mildews on tools and clothes. Keep up seaweed sprays for brown rot and other problems.
- December is the beginning of the serious fruit fly season. Make sure your traps are kept topped up with bait. if you haven't already done so, place cans of repellent near tomatoes and fruit crops. Pick all ripe fruit and vegetables.
- Grasshoppers may be a problem now, as green grass dries off. See pp. 113-17.
- Pick fruit infected with brown rot at once. For sprays, see pp. 136-39.
- Make sure fruit is checked once a week for codling moth damage. Pick out infected fruit at once.
- Dust under grape vine leaves with powdered sulphur, or use half strength bordeaux spray for downy mildew.
- Plant beans now in aphid-prone areas; late plantings are less susceptible.

INDEX

By the same author:

Organic Control of Household Pests
Illustrated with many black and white
drawings and full-colour photographs.

Published November 1988
Reprinted July and October 1989
ISBN 0 947214 02 X
Recommended Retail Price $13.95

Jackie French

**Organic Control of
Common Weeds**
Illustrated with many
black and white
drawings.

Published 1989
ISBN 0 947214 06 2
Recommended Retail
Price $13.95

A-Z of Useful Plants
Illustrated with full-colour photographs.

Published 1990
ISBN 0 947214 07 0
Recommended Retail Price $14.95

Available from all good booksellers, or
direct from the publishers:

Aird Books Pty Ltd
PO Box 122
Flemington, Vic. 3031